The Problem
Clergymen Don't Talk About

The Problem Clergymen Don't Talk About

by
CHARLES L. RASSIEUR

THE WESTMINSTER PRESS
Philadelphia

Book Design by Dorothy Alden Smith

Published by The Westminster Press®
Philadelphia, Pennsylvania

PRINTED IN THE UNITED STATES OF AMERICA

9 8 7 6 5 4 3 2

To
Ginni, Ted, and Bill
for
their patience and faithfulness

Library of Congress Cataloging in Publication Data

Rassieur, Charles L   1938—
  The problem clergymen don't talk about.

  Includes bibliographical references.
  1. Pastoral counseling. 2. Clergy—Sexual behavior.
I. Title.
BV4012.2.R33   253.5   75–40306
ISBN 0–664–24790–3

I REMEMBER in seminary there were stories in pastoral counseling about keeping your door three inches open and your phone off the hook, and of all these frustrated women who are out to seduce the preacher. Unfortunately, you weren't told how to deal with women, but you were sort of given the impression that you don't want to help the woman, you just want to protect yourself, your own reputation, your future, and the whole bit. So those were the kinds of things that really were not very helpful at all.

A Protestant clergyman

CONTENTS

PREFACE

THE AIM OF THIS BOOK is to help clergymen cope more effectively, more confidently, and with a sounder theological understanding when they are sexually attracted to a female counselee or parishioner. There is no intention that this book should be the final word or the authoritative answer on how pastors handle their sexual responses to women. On the contrary, the purpose will be best served if it facilitates a wider discussion of a problem clergymen ordinarily do not talk about, and if it gives pastors some fresh insights for working out better answers and strategies for their own pastoral ministries with women.

The following pages will draw mainly upon my own research interviews with parish pastors. While I was engaged in that research, I was often asked why I wanted to study how ministers handle their attraction to female counselees. It was in part because of my conviction that it is an important issue needing research. Without a doubt the subject is also quite personal for me. I have served three congregations as a pastor and counseled in six counseling centers. I have a firsthand acquaintance with what it means to be sexually attracted to a counselee, to be charmed by all the striking qualities of her femininity, and to be faced with deciding how best to deal with what I am feeling. If it serves no other purpose, my research has aided me in finding greater understanding of myself and clarification for my own counseling practice. So the material that follows is primarily my effort to share with fellow pastors what I have learned about a critical problem that I believe is very familiar to most of us.

The subsequent material will contain many case descriptions of the experiences of actual pastors. Of course I have changed names and sufficiently altered nonessential details to protect the identity of the pastors and their counselees. Before the interviews with each pastor were recorded, the men were asked to describe a situation in which their experience with a counselee or parishioner fit the following definition of sexual attraction:

> Sexual attraction is to be drawn toward, or even
> to like, the female counselee for reasons directly
> associated for you with her sex. In other words,
> was what attracted you to her directly related to
> her being a woman?

The pastors were not limited to describing experiences they had had with women in what might be termed strictly formal counseling situations. It has become clear that pastoral ministries may occur in even the briefest contact between a pastor and parishioner, such as after a service of worship or at a church dinner. A limited number of the instances reported by pastors included just such casual contacts. Pastoral counseling must be viewed in a broader context than a fifty-minute counseling session.

Obviously this book and the research data behind it would not be possible without the full cooperation of the pastors I have interviewed. It was essential that they be willing to trust my discretion in handling the sensitive personal information they reported to me about their professional conduct. In every interview that I had with a pastor, I was impressed with the sincerity and frankness with which private details and personal feelings were related from their counseling experiences.

The first chapter deals with my own theories concerning the principal dynamics that operate when a pastor is attracted to a parishioner or counselee. Readers may identify similar dynamics operating in their own ministries and thus deal with them more easily once they have been recognized. The second chapter develops a theological frame of reference, with a set of axioms by which a pastoral counselor may make decisions about his counseling with women. I wish mainly to point up the importance for pastors to use their theological resources in these situations, and I will suggest particular issues I feel especially require attention. The next three chapters will focus on the problems related to the three persons most directly involved with the pastor. In Chapter 3 the question will be how the pastor deals with himself regarding his sexual responses. The following chapter proposes possibilities for his consideration as he deals with the counselee. And in Chapter 5 we will review the question of how a pastor might handle this subject with his wife.

I have asked my wife, Ginni, to write Chapter 6. It will be the honest response of one minister's wife about what it means to her that her husband not only regularly counsels women but also is at times sexually attracted to some of them. I hope it will be helpful for pastors to read how another counselor's wife feels. Perhaps it will help them to appreciate their own wife's feelings. I hope, too, that what Ginni has written may be useful to other wives as they look for clarification of their own feelings about their husband's relationships with women.

My intention is to speak only to the experiences of male pastoral counselors. This is the case mainly because my own research has focused only upon male pastors and because I am obviously a male speaking from his own experiences. Also, I have the firm conviction that unquestionably it would be inappropriate for a man by himself to attempt to comment upon or analyze the sexual responses of a female pastor. Such a task requires, in my opinion, a woman's viewpoint. Certainly we can no longer assume that pastors are all necessarily men; statistics from the major denominations indicate the day is soon coming when there will be a thousand or more ordained clergywomen. The whole matter of the female pastor's sexual response requires separate research and separate treatment. With that important limitation in mind, whenever reference is made to pastors or ministers, for the purpose of this book, I will be referring only to male clergy.

Two other limitations need also to be mentioned. We shall be considering only the experiences of Protestant parish clergymen. My research has not included any Roman Catholic priests. I feel that the uniqueness of their ministry would require a treatment separate from the work I have done. Obviously, Roman Catholic priests do function as pastoral counselors for their parishioners. However, in several important respects the priest's situation is different from that of the Protestant clergyman. Most notably, the priest has taken a vow of celibacy, and he is not in a marital relationship. Those facts alone suggest that a separate treatment would be necessary in order to understand the dynamics related to how priests cope with their sexual attraction to female counselees and parishioners.

It is also important to observe that this book will make no reference to the occurrence of homosexual attraction in pastoral counseling. We will examine only what takes place between the male counselor and the female counselee. The question of homosexual attraction is relevant and must be assumed to be critical for some pastors. But we shall have to wait for that issue to be dealt with elsewhere.

Within those limitations, my purpose is to address the male parish clergyman who serves a Protestant congregation. He certainly represents the majority of all ordained persons in Christian service. My research involved pastors with a wide variety of training in counseling, but all were serving local churches, and counseling was only one of the several functions for which they were responsible in the church. None of them was a specialist in counseling, and all took their pastoral responsibilities seriously. Those two characteristics, I believe, will identify them closely with other pastors who are equally concerned about the pastoral care they give their parishioners.

Of course, I am indebted to the many persons who have assisted in the initial research and the preparation of this book. Many of my ideas were refined and enlarged with the help of Howard J. Clinebell, Jr., David Griffin, Frank W. Kimper, and Allen J. Moore. The preparation of this book has been a constant reminder of my indebtedness to them for helping me bring some measure of coherence and conciseness to my research. Finally, as anyone knows who has ever tried to put his thoughts into a book, the deepest word of appreciation must be reserved for one's family and spouse. Ted and Bill have been patient with their father's preoccupation with the typewriter, and Ginni could not have been more supportive. I am particularly pleased that she has shared in this book with the chapter she has written. Our work together on the manuscript has helped us find deeper dimensions in each other's feelings as we continue to explore together what our sexuality means to each of us. I hope the pages that follow may help others, also, to find those similar dimensions in their own lives.

Now, with much gratitude to all who have helped me, I am glad to accept fully the responsibility for the shortcomings and errors that become evident to the reader.

C.L.R.

Harrisburg, Pennsylvania

1
The Dynamics
of a Common Pastoral Problem

> The right person pushes the switch and the whole
> body lights up, from the eyes into the brain and down
> through the chest and belly, and below that, too. It is
> the Child alone who lights up, and it either happens or
> it doesn't.—Eric Berne[1]

CAROLINE MITCHELL couldn't get out of bed when Pastor Somers came to call on her. She had phoned him at the church earlier to ask if he could stop by for just a few minutes. She was having her recurring back pains from a childhood accident. They were often so severe she had to stay in bed for days at a time.

Caroline was a lonely person. Her first marriage had been a tragic experience for her, her husband, and her four children. To ease that loneliness she had become more active in various programs of the church.

Since her divorce, Pastor Somers had come to mean a great deal to her. When the loneliness became overpowering, she knew she could unburden to him and have her problems met with understanding. Likewise, Pastor Somers had much genuine concern for Caroline. Not only was she a pretty woman, but he knew that life had been a hard struggle for her. He felt close to her in his pastoral relationship. He explained:

> There was a lot of understanding between us,
> you see, and some sharing of life on a pretty deep

level—the same kind of sharing that I experience
with my own wife. I care about her; I have a
pastoral concern for her. I care for her just as a
human being, as a beautiful person, and as someone to whom I'm attracted.

He had always tried to be discreet when calling on
Caroline at her home. The visits never lasted more than
thirty minutes, and were often briefer. On some occasions he was accompanied by other church members.
However, this particular day he was alone, stopping by
her house quickly on his way to make hospital calls.
Caroline had mentioned on the phone that the door
would be unlocked and he was to come in. He would
find her in bed.

As he walked into the bedroom it was all too clear to
him that he was much aroused sexually at that moment.
He thought to himself: She's a very attractive woman.
She's got a cute shape. To me, she is a kind of girl that
you think might be fun with in bed. But he had decided
long before that there would be limits to his pastoral
relationship with Caroline, and he had no intention
now of changing that decision.

As they talked he tried to clarify Caroline's situation for her. "Caroline, you have much love to give
and you need a man to return your love and com-
panionship. I cannot do that for you." Shortly afterward he left, saying he hoped she would be back on
her feet again soon, because all her friends were
missing her.

Later Pastor Somers reflected about his call.

There wasn't anybody else around, and it would
have been very easy to slip into something ro-
mantic. I'm sure I was trying to deal with those
feelings within myself by telling her, when she

> needed someone, that it couldn't be me. That
> was my way of handling it.

And about his sexual feelings as a person Pastor Somers added:

> I think my sexual attraction to Caroline and
> other women is a positive thing. I think maybe I
> would worry about myself if I weren't attracted
> to someone like that.

There are no statistics to tell us how many women go to ministers for counseling, but surely most pastors have more than a few women who come to them for help. We also know full well that pastoral counseling is not the only occasion when a minister associates with women in the church. It is not unusual for a pastor to have a female secretary who works beside him many hours of the week. Since women have assumed many more responsibilities in the local church, a pastor may have quite close and continuing relationships with a woman who is president of a church board or organization, a director of Christian education, a chairman of a committee, or just active in the church's life. It would be strange indeed if feelings of warmth and affection never arose.

Pastors are often attracted to women who are either about their same age or younger. However, it is not unusual for a minister to be attracted to a woman fifteen or more years older than himself. It is not possible to generalize about the relationship of time spent with a person and the attraction that may develop. Pastors have been attracted to women they have seen only occasionally as well as to women they have seen much more frequently. Attractions may occur in just one meeting or in situations involving long-term exposure. In other words, in almost any of the varied circumstances in which a minister sees or works with women as part of his usual pastoral routine he may find himself unexpectedly experiencing a strong sexual attraction to a woman.

A similar observation has been made by a psychiatrist writing in a journal for pastors:

> Whenever two people work very closely together toward a common goal with at least fair success, as a minister does with his parishioner, or a doctor with his patient, feelings of camaraderie and warmth almost inevitably arise between them.
>
> When the two people are of opposite sex and not too disparate in background, these warm feelings will almost always assume a sexual cast.[2]

That such feelings occasionally arise should come as no surprise, even to a pastor. They are natural. If they are understood, he may be able to cope with them and avoid more serious involvement.

PERSONAL PREFERENCE FACTOR

Researchers have been telling us about the psychology of human sexual selection for decades. Sexual selection means that each person is particularly attracted to certain features in the opposite sex while other features do not arouse strong attraction. Each person is unique, and that largely holds true when it comes to our sexual preferences. Although most men would agree concerning certain female features they find attractive, each person has his own particular likes and dislikes. Sometimes a man may be attracted to a woman who seems to be very much like himself, or perhaps he likes her because she is just the opposite of him in many respects. A man may be attracted to a woman who has many of the characteristics of his mother. Freud suggested that such an attraction is a rediscovery of mother.

> It is not without good reason that the suckling of the child at the mother's breast has become a model for every love relation. Object-finding is really a refinding.[3]

Or the woman may have a personality like the man's own ideal self-image, which he has not yet been able to achieve. Or a woman's particular physical features may fit closely his personal image of what feminine beauty should be. So, the theory goes, each man has his distinct preferences. Consequently Mary may really turn Sam on but leave Fred cold, because Fred and Sam have differing sexual tastes.

The process of sexual selection, of responding to one's own sexual preferences, works just as well in a pastor's study as in a dance hall or on a beach. A minister is not likely to be sexually attracted to every woman with whom he associates. But he will know it most definitely when he meets one who fits his personal criteria for feminine beauty! One pastor spoke of his attraction to a counselee because she was a blonde, and he knew that he had had a preference for blondes since high school days. Another simply noted that the counselee was big-busted, as his mother had been, and he felt that was a feature of special significance for him. In one case, a minister described his sexual response to the woman simply enough: "I am man; you are woman!"

It must be understood that this process of sexual attraction is basically unrelated to the degree of satisfaction a pastor feels about his own marriage. There are certain women to whom a pastor will be sexually attracted regardless of whether he is happy in his marriage or not. The experiences of many pastors were reflected by the comments of one in particular:

> My relationship with my wife was good at the time. In the last year our marriage has grown a great deal. Our sexual relationship by all means has been the best in the last year. So I wasn't running away from any bad situation at home. To explain how I felt, the thing I would have to go back to would be the physical characteristics of this woman, or any woman, that are just attractive.

There is no great mystery about the fact that ministers are sexually attracted to females. It is really the natural reaction of a man to a woman who has the characteristics that he prefers in a woman. Research interviews with pastors clearly show that they respond to beauty and charm the same as any other man. They are not insulated because they are pastors. Moreover, this response does not necessarily reflect some failure with their own marital relationship. Therefore it should no longer be regarded as noteworthy that ministers might be attracted to women who seek their professional help.

THREE SITUATIONAL FACTORS

There may often be more than one explanation why a pastor is attracted to a particular counselee. Besides the pastor's personal sexual preferences, there is evidence that at least three different situational factors may influence the intensity of a pastor's response to a woman.

Sexual subject matter. If a counseling session deals

with sexual matters, the counselor and perhaps also the counselee may find this arousing. David R. Mace, the prominent marriage counselor, was aware of this when he pointed out, "It should be recognized that discussion of sexual marital situations often stirs strong emotions, in the client and sometimes in the counselor as well."[4] Experienced ministers know that it is not out of the ordinary for a woman to talk about sexual matters during a counseling interview. One pastor related an experience that illustrated directly the point made by Mace.

A young couple with serious problems came to the pastor for marriage counseling. The pastor recommended that he see the husband and the wife individually for several sessions, since each of them had been unfaithful to the other. When the young woman came by herself, she talked openly of her feelings about sex as well as details about her affairs with other men. As the woman talked so much about her sexual feelings and activities, the pastor realized how interested he was becoming. He explained that "when a lot of the sexual material came out, I was listening hard and imagining myself involved in her situation. . . . My fertile imagination put me there with her." However, when the woman went on to talk about other matters, the pastor noted that his sexual interest abated. "My sexual attraction was because of her mention of the sexual material, and when she got all of this out of her system, that finished that. We were no longer talking about her sex life, and I no longer had those feelings."

Satisfying important needs. A second way counselors may be sexually aroused in a counseling situation is through the counselor's perception that he is helping to satisfy some of the woman's important needs. He may feel that the woman is dependent upon his help, his support and understanding, during her time of personal crisis. If a woman has a low image of herself, she may derive important strength from the counselor's affirmation of her as a person. The tip-off to a pastor that he is becoming aroused may be his awareness of his own strong feelings of sympathy accompanied with a desire to be protective of the woman.

Meeting a woman's needs and helping her to feel better about herself as a person and as a woman can arouse strong sexual feelings for a man. One pastor frankly said, "I have always been attracted to women who would at least play the game of needing somebody to protect them." Another pastor described the "certain satisfaction and gratification" he felt from the counselee's dependence upon him. The experiences of many pastors clearly suggest that the male psyche readily responds to a woman who needs a man's help.

Sexual availability. An equally important third way pastors are sexually aroused is their perception that the woman is sexually available to any man, or to the pastor in particular. Pastors may find themselves responding to what seems to them to be a signal, sometimes subtle and implicit, at other times overt and direct, to the effect that the woman would allow some kind of sexual intimacy if the pastor were to take any initiative. It must be clear that we are talking only about the pastor's perception. A pastor may be utterly mistaken about a woman's intentions. He may conclude she is trying to seduce him when in fact she is not. However, it is his perception of her availability that directly heightens his sexual interest in her.

Pastors have reported a variety of circumstances in which they perceived that a counselee was communicating her sexual availability. In some instances the woman has come right out and said so. Or if a woman has a history of sexual promiscuity with numerous men, the pastor may conclude she would be available to him also. In some cases a pastor may also come to this conclusion by more subtle clues, for example, the degree to which the clothing she wears reveals her physical features. Many pastors will be able to identify with the report of this particular clergyman:

> For the first session she was very demurely dressed. But at the second session she came in clothes that did more for her figure, and the third time she actually wore a transparent blouse. Maybe those things don't hit you right away, but sooner or later they register.

The Four Factors in Combination

We have been discussing four main factors that account for pastors' becoming sexually attracted to female counselees. The first related to a clergyman's own personal sexual preferences for particular characteristics in a woman's personality or her physical features. The other three were situational factors related to the nature of the counseling relationship. Experiences reported by pastors show that they are attracted to counselees when the discussion of explicit sexual matters occurs, when the pastor feels he is a source of important help and support to the woman, and when the pastor perceives that the woman will be sexually available if he wishes to make overtures.

The evidence suggests that if a pastor is attracted to a woman because she fits his preferences for beauty, any one of the three situational factors may intensify that initial basic attraction. Imagine what a pastor's sexual attraction to a woman might be if he is quite sexually attracted to her to begin with; and on top of that he perceives her as needing his help and strength, as being readily available to him sexually; and in addition, the counseling interviews are devoted mainly to a review of sex-related topics! In such a situation a pastor would be expected to experience a maximum degree of sexual attraction.

On the other hand, it is possible that although a pastor was initially attracted to a woman but none of the three situational factors occurred, he would more than likely experience a low level of attraction. The occurrence or absence of the three situational factors makes a considerable difference as to what a pastor really experiences toward a female counselee.

Awareness of the varying effects of these four factors and how they may influence a counseling relationship can greatly assist a pastor to cope more confidently with the situation. At least it may help him to identify whether his attraction is based upon the woman as a person or whether it is the situational factors that are intensifying his attraction. It can be quite an important and freeing insight for a counselor to observe, as one did, that it was simply the discussion of explicit sexual matters that was arousing him.

> If she hadn't talked so much about sex, I don't think I would have been attracted to her.

FROM PROFESSIONALISM TO INTIMACY

Whenever a counselee comes to her pastor, there is the implicit assumption on the part of both persons that the relationship is basically a professional one. The minister is viewed by the lay person as a specialist with training that he can use to bring some kind of assistance to her problem. Even if the parishioner and pastor are close friends, the professional dimension generally implies that there are certain limits to the degree of intimacy the professional relationship will allow.

For example, some ministers define the professional relationship by being careful never to address the counselee by her first name. Many pastors maintain an explicit professional relationship by sharply limiting any physical contact to nothing more than a brief handshake. Others make it a practice always to counsel from behind a desk. The purpose in all these instances is clear; the message the pastor intends to communicate is that he is a professional person and the relationship —even if between two close friends—has a professional purpose. Without some such standards, serious problems can easily arise.

One pastor described his relationship with a counselee, which extended over a number of years and was characterized by a breakdown in professional standards. The relationship began professionally enough, but it ended in intimacy between two persons in love with each other. The pastor reflected on the transition that occurred and said it was imperceptible to him at the time, like "slow erosion." But as he reconsidered what had happened, he could recognize definite clues that revealed how the relationship was becoming more intimate.

The first indication that the matter was getting out of hand was when subtle messages of a more intimate quality were communicated in both direct and indirect ways. He recalled that this type of communication was mainly at her initiative. The pastor described a meeting at which a number of persons were preparing to make evangelism calls.

She would look at me in such a way that I knew
she was seeking to communicate something. It
was a manipulative device on her part. Sometimes, at a moment of seriousness in a group, she
would come by and just whisper something like,
"I love you," which would be certainly disarming
at the moment.

A second indication that their relationship was moving into a more intimate basis was the desire of both the
pastor and the woman to keep their relationship going.
Their need to hold on to each other was experienced by
both as a fear of rejection. So, invariably when there had
been a span of time when they had had no contact, one
or the other made a purposeful attempt to reestablish
the relationship.

When I would decide to be a faithful pastor and
cut this thing off, I would go for a week or ten
days and not see her. I would feel very badly.
Either I would call her up and say, I want to talk
to you, or she would stop in the office and say
something which would tell me—or I would be
telling her—that we needed to relate. And this
kept going on.

Another clue that the pastor recognized was the
woman's unusual eagerness to offer revelations to him
about her past sexual experiences. This warning signal
the pastor missed, but he suggests that pastors should be
alert to it.

Beware of a woman who comes in and immediately shares with you that she's had intercourse
with fifteen people, and what do you think of
that. This particular woman was quite exhibition-
ist in terms of sharing her hang-ups and her feelings. She brought out sexual material quite soon

> in the counseling. One thing to be aware of is a person who too quickly divulges her sexual experiences, fantasies, or exploits.

A fourth clue was what the pastor experienced within himself. In retrospect this pastor saw how he chose to allow himself to be manipulated by the woman's interest in him.

> I was willing to sacrifice my standards and my personhood for her, by allowing myself to be controlled by her feelings. I surrendered who I was. I think that the fulfillment of my relationship with her meant more to me than my integrity.

This willingness to be manipulated occurred in the pastor even though a psychologist told him that the woman almost always relates to other persons as a child. In the language of transactional analysis, the pastor explained that, instead, it was he who related to the woman as a child relates to a mother.

> I did the things and made the responses that would be from son to mother, child to mother, as against plugging in my adult.

The pastor suggested that a clue to this kind of dynamic is the pastor's need to maintain the relationship. Out of his own experience he offered this warning:

> If the pastor needed her to see him, that would be a sign that he was going under, losing his own personal identity.

This pastor also thought a fifth clue could be related to his frustrations about his own marriage. Again, reflecting on his own experience, he observed:

> One of the bad signs is when you don't feel that you can take all of your woes and cares home but have to have an outlet somewhere else. You are

vulnerable when you are not able to fulfill yourself at home.

In his own case he had made this observation about
himself: When his relationship at home was good he
would seek to do something to disrupt it! As he explained, it was as if he needed to be sure he had a poor
marriage in order to justify to himself his intimate involvement with the parishioner.

The sixth clue to a changing pastor-parishioner relationship, according to the pastor, relates to the matters
of setting limits to the length of counseling sessions and
the frequency of telephone calls between the pastor
and the parishioner. At the outset of his own relationship with the counselee the telephone calls were few
and short, but when the relationship became more involved the calls could occur as often as every day. Both
he and the counselee called each other. They talked
sometimes from forty-five minutes to an hour. Obviously, when the longer phone conversations were occurring, he was not setting any limits on the length or
the frequency of the phone calls. Observing that long
counseling interviews are an important indication that
a professional counseling relationship may be breaking
down, the pastor commented:

When a pastor is, or allows himself to be, sucked
into talking to somebody for two, three hours at
a time, the red light is blinking.

LIMIT-SETTING IN PASTORAL COUNSELING

Desmond Morris has suggested that there is a regular
pattern to increasing human intimacy. The twelve steps
outlined by Morris follow a progression: (1) eye to body,
(2) eye to eye, (3) voice to voice, (4) hand to hand, (5)
arm to shoulder, (6) arm to waist, (7) mouth to mouth,

(8) hand to head, (9) hand to body, (10) mouth to breast, (11) hand to genitals, and (12) genitals to genitals.[5] Sexual attraction is the motivating energy that prompts such a progression. Unless interrupted at some point along the way, sexual attraction would ordinarily progress to the final stage of intimacy, which is sexual intercourse. In this context we see the singular importance of setting adequate limits so the progression is effectively interrupted before the relationship ceases to be professional.

One important way to set limits upon a counseling relationship is to prescribe the length of individual sessions. However, many pastors often fail to take the initiative to end the counseling sessions with women to whom they are attracted. One pastor reported that his sessions with a woman were about an hour and forty-five minutes in length and always lasted until the woman said she was ready to leave. The pastor thinks his failure to set time limits was related to his false confidence.

> I was so cocksure in myself, I didn't think to set any limits when I started with her. In fact, I was elated that this educated, musically gifted, and financially well off woman would seek my help. I had blown up as big as a dirigible.

And another counselor attributed his reluctance to end a counseling session to his lack of courage.

> I am aware that this session lasted longer than it should have. I was not aware that it had lasted as long as it did because I felt involved with her. I guess I didn't have enough guts to say, "Hey, that's enough for today."

There are other ways to set limits upon the counseling relationship besides definite ending times. To stop the counseling, or to make a referral to another counselor, sets a permanent limit upon the pastor's relation-ship with the counselee. Some pastors set limits by refusing to engage in long telephone calls or by insisting that calls be made only to the office. Other pastors dis-courage lengthy discussions of sexual topics. Effective limits are also established by arranging counseling ses-sions at a specified frequency, such as once a week or once every two weeks. If a pastor, for whatever reasons, decides not to employ some definite limits in his coun-seling with women, he will be failing to use a principal means for maintaining a professional helping relation-ship.

SUPPORTS FOR A PROFESSIONAL RELATIONSHIP

Why do some pastors become intimately involved with a counselee, allowing their affection for the woman to obscure the original purpose of the rela-tionship? Why, on the other hand, do other pastors draw a sharp line and say no despite convenient op-portunities for sexual intimacy? This is a complex is-sue, and to take a look at it we shall consider some important relationships. Data from pastors who have been interviewed point clearly to five main factors that singly or together support pastors in their efforts to maintain professional relationships and avoid op-portunities for sexual intimacy with a counselee. We have already reviewed the four main factors that in-tensify a sexual attraction to a female counselee. Those four factors must be effectively balanced by one or all of the following five factors if a profes-sional relationship is to be maintained.

Marital satisfaction. Many pastors have made it very clear that a good marriage in the parsonage does not rule out sexual attraction in the pastor's study. By the same token, a pastor's attraction to a counselee does not mean that his marriage is necessarily unstable or unsatisfactory for him. Pastoral counselors agree that they would have been attracted to the woman regardless of how well they were getting along with their wife at home. The comments of three ministers illustrate this point.

> Even if I was having the best of relationships with my wife, maybe I'd still be attracted to this woman. I don't know, it's a good possibility.

> I would be sexually aroused again regardless of the marital situation.

> Dressed the way she was, she would have been attractive no matter what kind of state of sexual satisfaction I was in at the time.

So the important issue is not the occurrence of sexual attraction, but rather how the counselor deals with it when it does occur. Although their satisfactory marriages did not prevent a sexual attraction to a counselee, married pastors felt that their satisfactory marriage either did help them cope effectively or that, had they had a good marriage at home, it would have aided them considerably. The following comments underscore how pastors saw the relationship between their marriage and their handling of the counseling situation.

> I feel I was able to accept my feelings better because of my good relationship with my wife. Feeling more secure in my marriage, which by this time was three or four years along, made it easier for me to accept the feelings I was having toward the counselee.

I really believe that I'm capable of handling potentially sexually laden difficulties largely because I have a very sexual, attractive relationship with my wife. If that relationship were not strong, fulfilling, satisfying, and healthy, then I would find it very difficult, I am sure, because of the kind of intimate relationships that I have in counseling situations. If it was an unhappy relationship at home, unfulfilling and unattractive, and with a lot of hassle, then I would find it far more difficult to deal with potentially very attractive situations.

A pastor who was going through some definite problems with his wife felt that this made a difference in the way he responded to the counselee.

If everything had been going great at home, it would have helped me to handle it, I think, much better. Some of that attention the parishioner has given me would still give me some measure of attraction, turn-on, or whatever you want to call it. I think it would still be there, but I wouldn't be so conscious of being in a bind or in a temptation situation.

Another pastor summed up the relationship between his marriage and his counseling with women by saying simply,

If I'm sick at home, I'm going to be sick, I'm afraid, somewhere else.

Fear of social consequences. Another factor that may be an important influence upon a pastor is his expectation of unfavorable or catastrophic reactions by other significant persons if he were to seek an intimate, nonprofessional relationship with the counselee. His wife's negative reaction may be a considerable deterrent in this respect. But even if the pastor's marriage is so very unsatisfactory that his wife's reaction would make little difference to him, there are other risks: the risk of scandal in the community, the condemnation of his parishioners, or the censure of ecclesiastical authorities.

One counselor was especially concerned about not risking the counselee's disapproval of him if he made known his feelings to her.

> My effectiveness as her counselor would have gone. At this time I think she would lose confidence in my ability to help her because in some of the counseling sessions that we've had, she has said that other men have been attracted to her and tried to make her, and it's simply turned her off—this is completely repulsive to her.

The risk of social consequences was a serious factor for one pastor who did not want to tell the counselee of his feelings for her. He reasoned that if he told her, she would tell others, and he was certain his job would be in jeopardy. Another pastor who had a strong attraction to a woman felt that the social risks and threat to his profession would not be worth the involvement. He says he is more settled in his life at age sixty-two than a young man, perhaps, so there are more aspects to his life now he wouldn't want to throw away for another woman.

> I am much less likely to go off the deep end in a counseling situation with an attractive woman than a younger man in his thirties. My way of life, the way I want to live, my feeling of security, my relationship to what I want out of life are all at stake. In the perspective of the other interests, involvement with a female counselee has too little to offer me at my age to make me take the risk.

Self-image as a pastor. The pastor's concept of himself as a professional person may be significant in his consideration as he decides about his relationship with a woman to whom he feels attracted. Pastors indicated this kind of professional discipline can take several different forms. In one case a Methodist pastor was guided by John Wesley's advice about avoiding unduly long pastoral calls.

> John Wesley says to finish your business and go. On occasion I will take longer and have coffee, not adhering strictly to Wesley's admonition, because I don't quite agree with him. But I keep a fairly busy schedule, so my other commitments don't allow me to stay much longer than the brief time I spent with this woman.

For another pastor the issue of professional behavior focused on his responsibility as a counselor to let nothing get in the way of fulfilling that calling.

> The counseling setting is for me an attempt to try to be totally and consciously with the other person where the person is. And if there are things that impinge upon me and keep me from trying to be with the person as completely as I possibly can, then I try to set those aside.

Theological and moral convictions. Many pastors described the theological or moral restraint they felt within themselves regarding their feelings and behavior toward a counselee. They related their theological struggles with familiar Scriptural sources about adultery in both the Old Testament and the New Testament. A pastor's moral conscience may be the principal influence to inhibit his behavior toward a woman. One pastor acknowledged why he could not become more involved with a woman in his church to whom he was strongly attracted.

This would be something that would grieve my Savior. And he gives me power, the strength, not to do it. I know if I didn't have his strength and his power working to give me the new life he wants me to have, I would be in her bed as quickly as possible.

Another man commented on his strong fear of adultery associated for him with his feelings toward a counselee.

Theologically I'm influenced by Jesus' words about whoever looks on a woman to lust after her has committed adultery with her in his heart. That's some of the root of my guilt. So, at that point, the relationship with Jesus and his words definitely affects how I felt about the feelings I had of attraction to her.

Still another pastor added:

I guess I go back to the Biblical teaching about adultery and the New Testament passage about lusting in your mind. I take this fairly seriously; this is something not to be done. Also in the back of my mind is the idea of the thought leading to the deed.

One clergyman found himself in a situation with a counselee in which they both had very strong feelings for each other. He felt certain that he could have taken advantage of the situation if he had wanted to. His restraint was not one of fearing social disapproval, but rather it was his own personal sense that it would have been wrong for him to have used the circumstances for his own satisfaction.

My feelings for her were strong enough and are strong enough that I would not want to do anything knowingly to hurt her. I think that was probably the overriding control on my emotions at the time, probably more so even than the expectations of my own marriage and of the church situation and the moral standards of society. You just don't kick somebody when she's down, particularly someone that you care very much about as I care for her.

Supportive social relationships. In several situations reported by pastors, it was clear they wanted purposely to obscure the pastor-parishioner relationship. They wanted the association with the counselee to be more of a relationship simply between two friends. This dynamic in pastoral counseling relationships suggests that if a pastor has a strong unmet need for nurturing, understanding, or camaraderie, he may turn the counseling situation with all its built-in opportunities for intimacy into a situation for himself to receive the interpersonal support he has missed from other relationships elsewhere.

This seemed to be the case with a pastor who saw himself in something of a vocational crisis around his identity as a pastor. He wanted to overcome the distance he felt between himself and the people in his church so they would not see him on a pedestal. This was part of his motivation when he went to see a woman in her home to deal with a marital problem. Her husband was away at the time, but it was by mutual agreement with the husband that the pastor had arranged to see the woman alone. Shortly after he arrived, he made it clear to her that he wanted a more informal relationship. As her pastor he felt their former way of relating had maintained too much distance.

> The style that I chose that evening grew out of assessing my own situation, which was pretty desperate. There was nothing to lose. I had approached her as a pastor, I had given her a lot of

the generalities and platitudes, and that didn't
seem to help. So I thought, I'll just go over there
as a friend and listen and take whatever comes.
I remember that particular night. I told her as I
had told her previously—but much more directly
—to not call me "Reverend" because I was more
concerned about being her friend than I was
about being her father figure, her priest.

The pastor recalled that the session ended several hours
later with the two of them kissing at the door and being
aware of their strong affectional feelings for each other.

Another clergyman has described his association with
a parishioner. She is his age and comes to the church
office to work and talk with him at least once a week,
sometimes more often. They talk for forty-five minutes
or an hour. He enjoys it because she is one of the few
persons who comes to him asking for advice who is
willing to listen to what he has to say. The woman does
things for the church. She takes initiative in such a way
that the pastor feels better about his own self-identity.
He says of her, "That kind of supportiveness, I think,
adds value and esteem to your own self-identity, like
what kind of person am I." He also adds about the
parishioner:

She's really a swell person, and I really like her.
I think she's efficient, helpful, and supportive. It
is just a real good feeling to be supported.

Pastors need to be involved in satisfying interpersonal relationships with a variety of interesting persons. Such relationships should include occasions for
fun, informal relaxation, friendly competition, and a
time for listening to one another. If a pastor feels isolated from such human contact, or if he feels isolated
from persons who genuinely care for him, unwittingly

he may be drawn by those needs into an intimate relationship with an attractive parishioner. The pastor who has satisfying friendships with a wide variety of persons will be less likely to use a professional relationship to meet his important unmet needs for interpersonal nurturing.

SUMMING UP

From what we know about how pastors relate to their female counselees we may emphasize several conclusions. It is clear that a pastor will be sexually attracted to a woman if she fits his personal sexual preferences for beauty and charm, both physically and in terms of her personality. Furthermore, this attraction can occur regardless of how satisfied a pastor may feel about his own marriage.

There are three important situational factors that may occur in the process of the counseling to intensify or perhaps even initiate the counselor's sexual interest. One is the discussion of sexual material, ideas, or details. This happens when a woman is describing problems of a sexual nature in her marriage or her past sexual experiences. The pastor may perceive that the woman is sexually available to him. He may draw that conclusion from subtle clues, such as the way she dresses, or if her life-style suggests she is promiscuous. A third factor accounting for a counselor's sexual interest is his perception that the woman is dependent upon him, needs his support or protection, or that he meets some of her essential needs for self-approval or self-affirmation as a woman and as a person.

It is self-evident that sexual attraction by itself, without appropriate restraints, will lead to increased intimacy. As long as the pastor experiences such attraction, limits will have to be set in order to preserve the professional relationship. We have concluded that five factors may be involved in a pastor's decision to maintain those effective limits.

The pastor's satisfactory marriage does not prevent an attraction, but it is often an invaluable resource in helping the pastor to cope and set effective limits. Fears of negative reactions from the counselee, his wife, or persons in the church may strengthen a pastor's resolve to maintain a professional counseling relationship. The pastor's own concepts of being a good pastor may be quite influential. His personal theological and moral principles are an invaluable source of support. Finally, if a pastor is being adequately affirmed and nurtured in a variety of interpersonal relationships, he will be less likely to seek to satisfy those important needs where he feels a strong attraction to a counselee.

Effective coping with sexual attraction requires an understanding of the dynamics at work in a particular counseling situation. With this outline of the factors influencing sexual attraction, pastors may see their own experiences from a new perspective. It can be freeing for them to realize what forces within themselves and what factors in the counseling situation aroused them. Also, pastors may decide with fresh determination to intensify work on their own marital relationships so they can be better equipped to deal confidently with their attraction to other women. Pastors may also be helped by examining their own life-styles in terms of where they are receiving personal affirmation and understanding of themselves. The cultivation of new friendships may help pastors to avoid seeking the fulfillment of those human needs with sexually attractive counselees.

But it is not sufficient for a pastoral counselor to have a firm grasp on psychological dynamics. Pastoral counseling is a theological enterprise and should be practiced under the discipline of theological reflection. We will now examine a theological approach to the issues of coping with a pastor's attraction to a female counselee.

2
The Pastor's Theology
for Coping

The Serpent was not wholly to blame; had Eve walked
away, she would not have heard his beguiling words.
—Morton Hunt[6]

"OH, I ALMOST FORGOT. Someone is coming in today."
Pastor Akers suddenly remembered he had a counseling appointment in fifteen minutes as he reached into
his shirt pocket for his calendar book. "Renee Holmes?"
he mused. "I can barely picture who she is. I think I saw
her a year ago at her mother's funeral."

Then his thoughts overtook him again about his problems at home. What else did he ever think about? It was
a constant preoccupation. Lately he had been forget-
ting quite a few things because of his worries about his
marriage. The seventeen-year-old union was practically
in a shambles. It was tearing his insides out to continue
living under the same roof with his wife. He knew it had
to be affecting the children, though they put on a brave
front.

His study door opened a crack and his secretary
poked her head into the room. "Pastor, Mrs. Holmes is
here for her appointment." "Oh," he muttered, still
thinking about his children and feeling guilty for what
they must be going through. "Yes, have her come in,

please," he replied as he quickly straightened some of the loose papers on his desk. He thought, How can I help anyone, Lord, when I've got so many problems myself?

What occurred in the next two minutes left Pastor Akers in utter disbelief. A young woman with a distinctively appealing figure walked through the door, closed it quietly, and walked over to him. "Pastor," she said with determination, "my problem is lust, and believe it or not, I am in love with you." And with those words as an introduction, she threw her arms around the shocked clergyman.

Pastor Akers made all the appropriate protestations, asserting that he had no such feelings for her. A week later there was a similar shower of affection upon the pastor from Mrs. Holmes. Again he registered his protest, but with a little less vigor than the week before. The next week there was more affection for Pastor Akers, but there were no more protests from him.

Although his marriage recovered some of its earlier stability, his intimacy with Mrs. Holmes followed a roller-coaster journey for over three years. Later he declared that he knew firsthand what it was like for Dr. Zhivago, being in love with two different women in different ways at the same time.

How can we formulate an adequate theological understanding of Pastor Akers' experience? He was a man suffering with a distressing marriage, being offered love and affection from an attractive woman. Does it make any sense to talk about his freedom and his responsibility under such extenuating circumstances? Was he not perhaps simply the victim of compelling psychological facts of life like those outlined in Chapter 1?

No. In this situation it is not sufficient for a pastor to

be armed simply with enlightening psychological insights about heterosexual attraction. Although many pastors approach their daily duties without much theological reflection about their calling, they do so at their own peril. They neglect a basic dimension of their profession. Every task performed by a pastor is a theological task, and counseling is certainly no exception. Unquestionably a pastor's theology should make a difference to him about how he functions as a counselor. And when it comes to coping with his own sexuality, his theological reflection should illuminate whatever psychological understanding he has of his relationship to the counselee.

For some pastors their theological view of sexuality essentially prohibits acknowledging any attraction to a counselee. As one pastor put it:

> It was the spiritual training that I had. I think it was the Spirit of God within me which reminded me that this kind of attraction certainly was taboo so far as I was concerned if I were to allow it to develop. So even thinking about it was a sin because the Bible says, "Lust in your heart and you commit adultery." So I found myself asking God to remove this attraction because it would be hampering if it was allowed to exist and grow, and it would hamper my own spiritual life.

The theology of another pastor suggested to him that in the church human sexuality should no longer be a reality. Not only was he personally embarrassed by the strength of his own feelings of attraction but he was also embarrassed theologically. He explained:

> I guess that I am virtually a Gnostic in my belief that in the Kingdom of God, that is the church, any sexual distinction is abolished. Then you dis-

cover, as I did with this woman, that it is not
abolished. To abolish it means to make it impotent. When you realize it is still potent, then the
relationships that we have here in the parish and
in the body of Christ cannot allow complete freedom in the sense of license. In the Kingdom of
God there is neither male nor female, but I guess
this isn't the Kingdom of God.

Other pastors are especially influenced by the com-
mandment not to commit adultery and by Jesus' words
that lusting in one's heart is in effect an act of adultery.
One man summed up his theology on the matter as,
"Mt. Sinai in the background, 'Thou shalt not commit
adultery.' I immediately felt guilty, of course."

In contrast to personal theologies that prohibit the
pastor's feeling of attraction to the counselee, other
ministers speak of theological viewpoints that basically
allow acceptance of their sexual response to the counselee.

I think maybe the freedom that I've experienced
with my theology is unique. I can accept the feelings as my own, recognize them, and also know
that I have responsibility toward myself and
toward my feelings. I think that kind of perspective, which would be a result of my theology,
helps some. I go through this thing without a
huge burden of guilt, as though it's been a big no,
no kind of thing. I don't feel especially guilty
about it.

Another pastor linked a change in his theological orientation to his experience in a Gestalt therapy group. He
explained it this way:

This has been a part of my growth. I used to have
a great deal of guilt, but the Gestalt experience

helped me to realize again that the sexual function is such a beautiful thing, so much part and parcel of man's and woman's lives, and that God intended it to be this way. So it's one of the beautiful features of life.

One pastor has described how he openly acknowledged his sexual attraction to a counselee, telling her of his feelings when she said she was uncertain about her relationship with him. She had previously shared intimate details from her own life and past sexual experiences, so the pastor reasoned that since she had been so honest he would be honest also about his feelings. In this process his theology of Christian community was a significant factor. Regarding the nature of Christian relationships in the church, he says:

The Christian community is built upon relationships that are honest, authentic, open, and trusting between persons. So to me my behavior in dealing with this problem with this woman would be grounded in that kind of Christian community. Biblically, I see the Christian community arising out of, and being nurtured and enriched by, the most authentic kind of human relationships that people are able to enter into. The fewer the games that are played, the fewer dishonest areas, the fewer pretenses there are, the better the relationship, and ultimately the better the community will be.

Unquestionably there can be many viable theological approaches to an understanding of human heterosexual attraction. But whatever a counselor's theological orientation may be, there are some issues unique to heterosexual attraction of which the pastor should take account in his theology.

TWO KEY ISSUES

Certainly one key issue with several important implications is the matter of personal responsibility where sexual attraction is concerned. We have already discussed the particular psychological dynamics that occur when a pastor is sexually attracted to a counselee. The implication is that such dynamics may preclude or eliminate the pastor's real freedom of response and choice. Psychological dynamics must not be confused with laws of behavior under which the person exercises no freedom as a choice maker. The most prevalent example is that of behavior modification, which suggests that man may be manipulated with the right use of positive rewards. Reduced to absurdity, this view proposes that man is fundamentally a robot absolutely controllable by external stimuli.

A theology that allows radical freedom and responsibility does not ignore the dynamics of psychological probability. Such a theological view does not ignore that, given certain sets of conditions in the counselor's office, certain kinds of behavior may be highly probable. But such psychological facts do not alter man's more fundamental characteristic, namely, that in every instance he exercises freedom of choice in response to his environment.

Would such an assertion be true even under the most inhumane conditions of tyrannous control of the human spirit? We may confront that question with the well-known views of Viktor Frankl, whose writings reflect his efforts to survive the Nazi prison camps. It was in those circumstances of total deprivation of external freedoms that Frankl became convinced of man's fundamental freedom as a choice maker, which no one can take from him.

> Man is *not* fully conditioned and determined; he determines himself whether to give in to conditions or stand up to them. In other words, man is ultimately self-determining. Man does not simply exist, but always decides what his existence will be, what he will become in the next moment.
>
> By the same token, every human being has the freedom to change at any instant. Therefore, we can predict his future only within the large frame of a statistical survey referring to a whole group; the individual personality, however, remains essentially unpredictable. The basis for any predictions would be represented by biological, psychological or sociological conditions. Yet one of the main features of human existence is the capacity to rise above such conditions and transcend them. In the same manner, man ultimately transcends himself; a human being is self-transcending being.[7]

A related issue of equal importance is the question of what it means for two persons to be in relationship. More particularly, what does it mean for a pastor and a counselee to encounter each other as persons? Is it simply the temporary meeting of two strangers, or only a brief transaction between a professional and his client? Or are there theological dimensions to the nature of human relationships that must be taken into account? This question is raised not only with respect to the counseling relationship but also in regard to the counselor's relationship with his wife. Should not a theological view of the pastor's marriage offer some light as to how the pastor relates to his wife when he is also experiencing an attraction to a counselee? Whether a pastor considers himself liberal, conservative, or middle-of-the-road theologically, he needs to reflect upon the meaning of that theology for human relationships if he is to relate appropriately to both the counselee and his wife.

ONE APPROACH TO THE ISSUES

The following theological statement is offered as one viable framework for coping with heterosexual attraction. Within this framework the pastor may develop a stance toward the issues of responsibility, freedom, and relationships as he makes decisions regarding himself, the counselee, and his wife.

> The Christian is both radically free as a decision maker and radically responsible for himself as he is. He affirms his freedom as he affirms the givenness of himself. Both are facts that must be confirmed for the self in relationship with others, where the uniqueness of each person is encountered by the unique freedom and givenness of other selves.

Clinebell, writing in *Basic Types of Pastoral Counseling*, has rightly set the broad purpose of pastoral counseling within the theological framework of the purpose of the church, i.e., the increase of the love of God and the love of one's fellowman. This is properly enlarged, as Clinebell notes, to include helping persons to love themselves more fully.[8] Reconciliation is thus the primary theological task as love overcomes the fundamental feature of sin, which is alienation of man from God, one's neighbor, and one's own self. Health, wholeness, and salvation may all be viewed as principally the absence of alienation and the presence of reconciliation. In the context of the statement above, man experiences reconciliation when he is in responsible relationships with others. That is to say, when man is in relationships in which he is *with* and *for* the other in care and love without any loss of his personal identity or integrity as a freely choosing, radically responsible self. The person is whole who maintains his personal center while entering totally into intimate relationships with others.

To develop this theological approach further, the pastor will find the work of John Cobb highly informative. Cobb's view of the Christian man and the Christian structure of existence offers a valuable resource for understanding the nature of Christian responsibility. Although Cobb does not apply his view directly to sexuality in pastoral relationships, the implication of his thought for coping with heterosexual attraction is self-evident.

Cobb's philosophical orientation is toward the thought of Alfred North Whitehead. One of the important features of Whitehead's thought is that there is some element of self-determination or decision for every occasion of experience.[9] Our past experiences may sharply limit the range of the choices set before us, but Cobb emphasizes that man still chooses his response to the alternatives he finds before him. "What I have been in the past, and what the world as a whole has been, may narrowly limit what I can become in this next moment. But within those limits it is still my decision in that moment as to how I shall react to all these forces impinging upon me."[10]

Man's past and his environment obviously provide real limits to his range of choices. By the same token, an attractive counselee who fits the pastor's sexual preferences also sets certain parameters to his range of choices. But Cobb's assertion is that man in all instances exercises his own free choice of response to any situation. Cobb stresses both the real limits of any situation and the distinct human freedom within those limits. To speak of unqualified freedom without limitations would be absurd. The freedom available to man is his freedom to respond to the circumstances confronting him.[11]

This concept of human freedom and responsibility in any situation is developed further by Cobb when he explains what he calls the Christian structure of existence. Basically, the Christian is responsible for his total existence. He is not only responsible for his choices but also for the motives of his choices. In the Christian structure of existence the Christian is always responsible for what he is.

> We cannot simply accept what we are as the given context within which our responsibility operates. If I find that I am not a loving person, I must acknowledge my responsibility for not being a loving person; and if I find that I cannot even will to become a loving person, I must acknowledge responsibility for that failure of my will.[12]

To apply Cobb's point of view to the pastoral counseling situation, the counselor can never be said to be totally helpless; neither is the counselee absolutely helpless. Despite the reality of psychological influences for sexual attraction, from a Christian standpoint the element of personal choice, of freedom and responsibility, can never be absent for either the counselor or the counselee.

Concerned as a pastor is with the interpersonal relationship between himself and other persons, the work of Martin Buber must also be given consideration. One of Buber's most valuable contributions is his insight regarding the relationship of *I* to another self, a *Thou*. It is through such a relationship—in which each experiences the other while retaining his own concreteness—that the *I* affirms itself and grows stronger. "Persons appear by entering into relation to other persons."[13] If the counselee is to develop, she needs to be able to encounter another person. Self-discovery and self-possession, which are essential for finding identity, occur in the relationship where *I* encounters *Thou*.

There is a risk to this kind of encounter.

> This is the risk: the primary word (*I-Thou*) can only be spoken with the whole being. He who gives himself to it may withhold nothing of himself.[14]

This communication of one's whole being does not mean the loss of center, but rather being present in the totality of one's self. As Buber explains elsewhere, it involves inclusion so *I* participates with *Thou* without losing the distinction between *I* and *Thou*.[15]

Pastors will particularly take note at this point of Buber's assertion that it is in the encounter of the *I* with the *Thou* in the interpersonal relationship that encounter with God, the eternal *Thou*, also occurs. If the counseling relationship is not an encounter between two persons present to each other in their total being, then the possible indwelling of the Present Being is jeopardized between them.[16]

The pastoral counselor may also be informed by Paul Tillich's insights about freedom and responsibility in relationships. Tillich has identified pairs of elements that constitute the basic ontological structure. One of those polarities is that of individuality-participation, which states the ontological fact that self-identity, self-centeredness, requires encounter and participation with another person. "No individual exists without participation, and no personal being exists without communal being. The person as the fully developed individual self is impossible without other fully developed selves."[17]

Tillich also demonstrates how freedom and destiny are mutually dependent upon each other, for "only he who has freedom has destiny."[18] Destiny forms the conditions and limits to freedom and is not the opposite of freedom. Destiny is the given from which our decisions arise in freedom. Destiny is the concreteness of everything that constitutes the person's being, which is the basis of the person's freedom. That freedom is based on the responsibility of the person to answer for all his decisions, for in man's freedom "his acts are determined neither by something outside him nor by any part of him but by the centered totality of his being."[19]

THEOLOGICAL IMPLICATIONS FOR PASTORAL COUNSELING

In the light of the views of Frankl, Cobb, Buber, and Tillich we may draw conclusions about the uniqueness of man. This uniqueness is derived in large measure from the fact that man cannot attribute responsibility for his choices to anyone or anything outside himself. Certainly this is the case for the Christian man. Circumstances may and do sharply limit his range of choices, but they do not eliminate his freedom to choose. Before God the Christian is responsible for all his choices,

choices that basically determine his being and his behavior. If man is not free, it is meaningless to talk of his
responsibility. Tillich asserts that man has a destiny because he is free. Cobb's analysis shows that the Christian
is radically responsible for who and what he is in the
Christian structure of existence.

We are therefore led to the following observations
regarding human heterosexual attraction. Such attraction is often regarded as totally compelling in certain
situations. However, in the final analysis we must maintain that the person freely chooses—in some cases
choosing to regard a situation as totally compelling and
himself as helpless—and by such a choice he exercises
his personal responsibility. The Christian's responsibility is not lessened in any way in an erotic or sexually
stimulating situation.

Secondly, pastoral counseling must also take account
of the ontological and theological potential in an interpersonal relationship. The analysis by Buber and Tillich
is persuasive that the development of an individual requires an encounter with another person, an encounter
that is communication of being with being. The counseling relationship, around whatever issues, that is de-
void of such personal communication is lacking the feature essential for the counselee fully to discover herself
as an individual. Moreover, as Buber points out, anything less than a dialogical relationship sharply limits
the possibility of any encounter with God through the
relationship.

With these theological considerations in mind, is it
possible to outline a specific value framework for dealing with the counselor's attraction to a counselee? If
that is to be attempted, something more is required
than just a set of rules to fit a wide range of possible

counseling situations. The primary question is not how ministers can stay out of trouble when they feel turned on. A far more significant question is whether heterosexual attraction felt by the counselor can be an occasion, even an opportunity, for facilitating the potential in an *I-Thou* encounter. If we miss that opportunity, then we run the real risk of blocking the kind of interpersonal dialogue necessary for the counselee's own self-discovery and personal growth. If the attraction experienced by the pastor actually hinders communication from the center of one person to the center of the other, it will be a serious obstacle to the constructive potential of the relationship. Moreover, it will be a violation of the individuality of each person. It will also jeopardize the possibility for the counseling relationship mediating any genuine encounter with the eternal *Thou.*

A VALUE FRAMEWORK FOR THE COUNSELOR

1. *He acknowledges and accepts all his personal feelings, fantasies, and impulses of sexual attraction.* For the counselee to have the maximum opportunity for self-discovery and self-knowledge, the counselor must accept his own total experience in the relationship so he can fully communicate as one being to another. Carl Rogers has stated this principle in the context of his concept of "congruence."[20] Openness to oneself as being and person is essential for being open to the other person. If the counselor fails to accept his own experience, he jeopardizes the creative possibilities of the encounter. As Buber said: "Only when two say to one another with all that they are, 'It is *Thou,*' is the indwelling of the Present Being between them."[21]

This axiom is also rooted in Tillich's observation about the polarity of freedom and destiny. If the pastor is to be a centered partner in the relationship, fully responsible for his free choices, he must accept the destiny of what is given about himself, his concreteness as a being. This must obviously include the pastor's sexuality and his sexual responses to the counselee. To the extent the counselor fails to accept what is given about himself as a person, to that extent he limits his experience of freedom as deliberation, decision, and responsibility.[22]

2. *He distinguishes between feelings and behavior.* It would be a mistake to suppose that acceptance of one's feelings will determine one's conduct without having any choice about one's own behavior. The pastor distinguishes between his feelings and his behavior because he accepts his feelings of sexual arousal without supposing they must or will lead to sexual intimacy with the counselee. Charles Kemp comments on this issue as he first quotes D. W. Orr.

> Dr. Orr, speaking of the counselor says, "He differs from the client, however, in being more aware of his needs and impulses, having them under greater self-observation and conscious control and, above all, knowing that they must find gratification in other relationships than those with clients."
> It is natural to like or dislike a person. If a counselor's feelings about a counselee become intense, it can create a problem. To see a woman as sexually attractive is one thing; to exploit that feeling or act upon it is another.[23]

From Cobb's viewpoint the Christian does not confuse his feelings with his behavior because to do so would be to identify the self with a particular aspect of the psyche. In the Christian structure of existence the Christian transcends every aspect of his psyche. If he does identify with some part of his psyche, he must take responsibility for having made that identification. Consequently, for the Christian, his free power of choice stands between the energy of sexual feelings and any behavior motivated by those feelings. No matter how strong such feelings may be, they never supersede the Christian's freedom and responsibility for his own choices.

From Tillich's analysis of the ontological elements, we see that there is no way to have destiny without freedom. Hence it is ontologically impossible for man to have the givenness of his feelings without also having the freedom and responsibility of his choices. If there is destiny without freedom, the polarity collapses. Each person's behavior is determined only by the centered totality of his being. "Each of us," Tillich affirms, "is responsible for what has happened through the center of his self, the seat and organ of his freedom."[24] Thus, because the counselor is free to choose his behavior, whatever the givenness of his personal experience, he accepts his experience because he has clearly distinguished between his feelings of sexual arousal and any behavior motivated by those feelings.

3. *Each person, counselor and counselee, is responsible for his or her own feelings and behavior.* Conventional wisdom would suggest that the dynamics of human sexuality are such that in some situations one may really be helpless to resist seduction. Cobb rightly declares that circumstances of a situation limit the possibilities within which freedom may be exercised, and certainly a situation conditioned by sexual stimuli necessarily limits the range of possibilities open to

choice. Nonetheless, the affirmation of the Christian's freedom of choice and his radical responsibility for himself requires that each person in the relationship accept final responsibility. Paul Johnson has pointed out the importance of personal responsibility for the goals of pastoral counseling:

> Personality problems hinge upon questions of responsibility.
> So in the problems of personality the needed growth is achieved in the development of new responsibility.[25]

The counselor's experience of sexual attraction is a unique opportunity to clarify and underscore the theological principles of Christian freedom and responsibility within a relationship. This can occur as the counselor either implicitly or explicitly declares that he, not the counselee, is responsible for his feelings of sexual attraction. That is to say, the counselor owns his feelings, does not blame the counselee for how he has responded to her, and declares that he is finally responsible for how he will deal with his feelings. As the counselee learns how the counselor takes care of himself and his own feelings, she has a theologically sound model for learning to be responsible for herself and her own feelings.

4. *Reporting the pastor's feelings enhances the dialogical process.* This axiom builds upon the responsibility of each person, stressed in the third axiom above, in the framework of the relationship. The context of clear personal responsibility allows a freedom with clear limits for open sharing of mutual feelings.

We misread Buber and his analysis of the ontology of the *Between* if we assume that just talking about feelings guarantees an *I-Thou* encounter. Buber says such an encounter may occur between persons who exchange no words.

> Just as the most eager speaking at one another does not make a conversation . . . so for a conversation no sound is necessary, not even a gesture. . . . For where unreserve has ruled, even wordlessly, between men, the word of dialogue has happened sacramentally.[26]

Buber is clear that communication must occur between the whole being of two persons, and he is equally clear that this is not assured simply by the occurrence of speech. The essence of dialogue transcends words and uses speech to accomplish its end.

Thus, this reporting of the pastor's feelings of sexual attraction is not to be viewed as an end in itself. In this sense it could conceivably be a violation of the dialogue. Rather, in the context of personal responsibility, the reporting of feelings is to occur in service of a true dialogue between counselor and counselee in terms of where each, as a centered being, is at the moment.

5. *Explicit limit-setting is integral to the counseling relationship.* This principle is widely recognized as an important aspect of the pastoral counseling relationship.[27] The Christian must assume his own responsibility for his part in an interpersonal relationship. He cannot give away any of that responsibility to the relationship itself. The centered self must define how it chooses to participate in the relationship. Only by this kind of definition can there be any encounter between *I* and *Thou*.

It is consistent with this point of view for a pastor to

assert clear limits that he wants to observe. Each counselor will choose his own limits, such as the length of time for counseling sessions and the circumstances in which the counselor will have further contact or conversation with the counselee. Failure to set limits that define the relationship would be an example of a choice by the pastor, regardless of whether it is conscious or unconscious, to have a different kind of relationship with the counselee.

6. *Consultation is an important resource.* Clinebell has spoken of the importance of the pastor's having his counseling reviewed periodically with a colleague or other experienced counselor.[28] From the theological viewpoint the Christian counselor must assume responsibility for the kind of counselor he is. It follows that he is responsible, in terms of his own freedom of choice, for choosing whether or not to avail himself of outside consultation that could facilitate his growth as a person and as a counselor. Such consultation would ostensibly aid the counselor in bringing a more thoroughly dialogical relationship to his counselees.

7. *The pastor's growing relationship with his spouse affects his counseling relationships.* The quality of marriage envisioned in this axiom is based upon a radical Christian responsibility that affirms each partner's personal freedom. Such a marriage will facilitate a dialogical relationship where the being of one partner truly encounters the being of the other partner. Wayne Oates has observed that "the Protestant pastor functions as a counselor within the context of his identity as a married man."[29] A marriage affirming each partner's freedom and responsibility will be a positive resource for the pastor as he copes with the occurrence of his sexual attraction to a counselee.

If a pastor's marriage is preeminently a dialogical relationship, there can be appropriate opportunities for a pastor to share with his wife the kinds of feelings he has toward a counselee. If husband and wife are open to each other's being, and if they affirm each other's freedom to be, the basic framework will exist for them to face the issue of heterosexual feelings each of them has toward other persons.

However, it must be clearly understood that no specific rules can be offered about when, how, and how frequently a pastor and his wife will discuss such matters. Any attempt to set rigid rules would be a violation of the dialogical principle. However, it is highly likely that a husband and wife who are truly open to each other will have occasions to discuss what it means to both of them that the husband experiences a sexual attraction to a female counselee.

COMMENTS ON THE SEVEN AXIOMS

Are these seven principles workable for the average parish minister? Or do they require more sophisticated training than is available to most pastors serving local churches? Experiences reported by parish pastors show that these are well within the range of their capability. One might wrongly suppose that only counseling specialists could be so open in expressing sexual feelings that can be so threatening to the counselor. Although it is quite true that there are some pastors who are unaccepting of such sexual feelings, there are many others who not only accept them but even allow themselves to enjoy them.

The personal reaction of many pastors to their sexual feelings is closely related to their theology of their own sexuality. Sexuality cannot be viewed simply as psychological, because it is a pastor's nature by training and profession to view his experiences through theological lenses. The question is whether the pastor has an adequate theology for relating the basic themes of the gospel to the common dimensions of being human. Pastors represent far-ranging theological positions, from a conservative Biblical literalism to the most liberal humanism. Whatever position a pastor takes, it is incumbent upon him to continue to refine his theological understanding of human sexuality. Failure to do so may cause the pastor to shortchange both himself and the persons with whom he counsels.

More apparent than anything else is the need for parish pastors to integrate their intellectual theology with their visceral humanity. It is not unusual to hear pastors say they feel quite conflicted because their heads rationally tell them one thing about their sexuality while their feelings somewhere below their heads send them quite different signals. Theology and feelings generated in counseling sessions need constantly to be integrated. Any theological viewpoint out of touch with basic life experiences, including sexuality, should be questioned as to whether it is really Christian.

There are perils in reporting the pastor's feelings as a contribution to the dialogical process. Whenever two persons talk about their feelings of sexual attraction for each other there is a normal tendency for their relationship to become more intimate and less formal. It is not sufficient just to talk about such feelings. The pastor needs to remember that the reporting of his sexual feelings must be done within the context of effective limit-setting if the formal pastor-parishioner relationship is to be preserved. Reports from pastors clearly show that where such limits have been absent, the relationship gets out of hand.

Are there times when a pastor should not report his sexual feelings to a counselee? When the counselee is dealing with an acute crisis, the dialogical process will probably be best served by avoiding reference to any of the pastor's feelings. In such cases the task is to deal with the immediate problem. Reporting a pastor's feelings, particularly sexual feelings, would in most cases be intrusive in crisis counseling. More will be said about this question in Chapter 5.

The fundamental assumption of the seven axioms is that man is free to make decisions and is responsible for what follows from such freedom. This view of the Christian man differs quite markedly from many theorists and from what is often assumed to be the general human experience. The conventional assumption says that in an erotic circumstance human freedom of choice is sharply limited or precluded. Research on human behavior seems to support this view because the actions of human subjects appears to be determined by independent variables.

But such a view of man is not persuasive, even when dealing with such a matter as sexuality. Theodor Reik, for one, challenges any notion of helplessness about "falling in love," which is a particular kind of sexual attraction.

> Does not the expression "falling in love" itself imply the suddenness and violence of the passion? We are inclined to think that it strikes a person like a blow, or that a person falls into love as into a trap. The first comparison is wrong, as

is also the second. There is no blow, no *coup de foudre,* even in love at first sight. All has been prepared. Nobody falls in love. He or she rather jumps into it. Really, the most you can say is that a person lets himself fall.[30]

Another writer, Erwin Wexberg, has made a similar observation: "We repeat again: human responsibility does not cease where human passion begins, because this is the very point where responsibility must be shown. We are responsible for our passions."[31]

It is the basic view of this chapter that the pastoral counselor may freely choose a response that facilitates rather than hinders his encounter as a person with the counselee as a person. We conclude this chapter as we began, with reference to Morton Hunt's study of persons who had had affairs. Hunt wondered how people ever got involved in an affair. His conclusion was that somewhere along the line they chose to let themselves become involved.

> The seemingly innocent persons who have temptation thrust upon them by Fate are thus usually not so innocent after all; knowingly or half-knowingly, they have connived at their own seduction. Even where the temptation seems to have been purely accidental, the outside observer can see unconscious volition at work in the unfaithful in the form of a refusal to avoid or remove one's self from a high-risk milieu or situation. The faithful husband who goes on a convention trip with a group of men he knows to have a taste for pick-ups or call girls has voluntarily put himself in the line of fire; he is to blame if he gets hit. The husband and wife who intend to be faithful, but make

themselves part of a social circle in which, it is rumored, there are mate-swapping and sexual parties, are willfully increasing the chances of "accidentally" being faced with temptation too great to resist. The Serpent was not wholly to blame; had Eve walked away, she would not have heard his beguiling words.[32]

3
The Pastor Deals
with Himself

Many pastors either deliberately suppress such attraction or, by reasons of personal dynamics, repress attraction. Those who acknowledge attraction gain ascendancy over the complexities involved and generally are able to deal with the problems involved.
—Thomas McDill[33]

MARY JANE started crying. Pastor Williams could sense she wanted to say something that was bothering her deeply. In the six weeks she had been coming for counseling he had learned pretty well when she was on the verge of expressing troubling feelings. Looking up hesitatingly, Mary Jane found the courage to say what she had been feeling for a long time.

"Pastor, I don't know how to say this, but I love you, and I want to marry you!"

Shock flooded through Pastor Williams, followed by a rising surge of anger. "Mary Jane," he blurted out, "this cannot be! I must admit that I, too, am very much attracted to you. I can recognize that now. I knew it was happening between us from the beginning, though I didn't want to admit it. But I have a wife and two children, and our relationship has to stop right now. This has gone far enough!"

Afterward Pastor Williams knew that his anger flared

because Mary Jane had confronted him with something he had wanted to pretend was not happening. But when the words left her mouth, the realization was a blunt awakening for him.

> Just like a burst of fireworks. I wonder today, if she hadn't said that she wanted me to marry her, whether I wouldn't have had relations with her.

In fact, Pastor Williams' anger with Mary Jane was primarily anger toward himself for trying to fool himself about what was really happening. When Mary Jane's announcement of her interest in him set off the "lights and bells," the full force of what was happening finally dawned on him. He said to himself, Good Lord, is this how far this has gone? Good old Pete in the next parish told me about his experience with one of his parishioners, and now about the same thing is happening to me. How far can one go without having his eyes open? How could you be so stupid? You are a stupid ignoramus!

Pastor Williams was finally forced by Mary Jane to face what he pretended was not there, namely, his own sexual intentions to become involved with her. "I was hiding one thing, my sexual feelings for her, in one part of my mind from another part of my mind. I think I was really planning to take advantage of this whole situation somewhere along the line."

Pastor Williams' experience is an all-too-common illustration of how a pastor may purposely choose to be blind to his own feelings because he foresees some advantage possibly coming to him in the future if he maintains his self-deception. In Pastor Williams' situation the woman was quite attractive and the same age as he. She had originally come to him seeking help for her marital problems. Besides being attractive, she also had a number of interests similar to his, so they found it easy to talk about subjects of mutual concern. In the midst of a marital crisis, the woman was upset and uncertain about the right course for her to take. Pastor Williams recalls: "The more she went on the more I could see that she was grasping for something to hang onto . . . it was more somebody to hang onto."

As the counseling sessions progressed Pastor Williams was aware of his increasing sexual interest in her. Her manner of dress flattered her figure. He was aware of his own fantasies about her, that ". . . she would really be somebody to be in bed with." These thoughts were accompanied with fantasies of sexual foreplay. He also felt he was receiving the definite message from her that she was attracted to him. There was a decided "between the lines communication" going on about their mutual sexual attraction. But Pastor Williams preferred to ignore the obvious signals till Mary Jane's announcement confronted him with all that was happening.

Such self-deception is always a possible alternative for a pastor. The only remedy for this kind of blindness is a personal intention to be brutally honest with oneself. This honesty must be practiced by serious examination of the dynamics occurring between the pastor and the counselee. In this situation the problem was not that he was having fantasies. He knew from the outset that he was sexually attracted to her. The problem was that he chose to ignore what his fantasies meant—they went unexamined.

If a pastor is prepared to be honest with himself, he will probably be able to acknowledge the presence of at least some of his sexual responses to a counselee. Often a trusted colleague or consultant can greatly aid his candor with himself about his feelings. Failure to be

honest about one's genuine sexual interest in the counselee may well end far less happily than did Pastor Williams' startling lesson.

EXAMPLES FROM THE EXPERIENCES OF PASTORS

It will never happen to me!

Other examples from the experiences of pastors show
how they often deal with themselves in handling their
sexual feelings toward parishioners. Pastor Gardner had
decided that he would never be strongly attracted to a
counselee; therefore it could never really be a problem
for him. He had been out of seminary for six years. In
that time he had had many opportunities for counseling
women in his church and working with them in other
activities. He had been aware on different occasions
that some of those women were indeed attractive. He
recognized their sexuality, but he dismissed it from his
mind. This was an issue he had heard referred to in
seminary, but he felt confident that it would never be
a problem for him. His relationships with women just
could not cause him any concern.

Therefore he did not give it a thought when Pat
stopped to talk with him for a few minutes after the
service of worship. She hinted that there were some
serious problems between her and her husband, so Pastor Gardner suggested a counseling appointment for
Tuesday morning. The pastor had known Pat for more
than a year, though there had really never been any
occasions for him to talk very long with her. She was
four or five years younger than he. He had noticed that
she was a pretty woman, but he had not really had any
particular feelings about her.

Tuesday morning at 10:30 Pat arrived for the counseling session. She began talking about how unsatisfactory her marriage was, practically from the first day. Her husband got what he wanted, but it seemed that her feelings didn't count for anything. A year or so into her marriage she had met a nice fellow at work and had had a brief affair that ended unhappily. She was scared now, not knowing what to do or which way to turn to get things straightened out with her husband.

As Pastor Gardner was listening to Pat's outpouring of her problems, he had a weird feeling. Hey, she turns me on! I wonder what's going to happen now?

The very thing he had concluded would never happen to him was happening. No doubt about it!

> I knew I was attracted to her emotionally, the way she talked, and physically, the way she looked. She wasn't strong and overbearing. Strong and overbearing women I have trouble with. That's not the kind that would turn me on. But Pat struck me right away in that session as the kind of girl I would ask out.

He was attracted to the passive quality about Pat because her passivity helped him to feel more masculine. His wife is more aggressive, so "at times I've not felt as masculine, as in control of the marriage, as I would like to be."

Pat's situation also suggested that, since she had already had one affair, it might be easy for her to become involved in another—with the pastor if he wanted it. "It would be very easy, probably, if I wanted to start something, that she would probably go along. That was my impression."

Two immediate thoughts came to the pastor's mind in that first session. He suddenly remembered a fellow pastor he had known who was asked to resign from his church because he got involved with a woman, and his wife divorced him. Secondly, he quickly reasoned that he had married his wife for some special reasons, and the grass is not always greener on the other side of the fence.

Probably his greatest learning from the experience was that he was more like other people than he had wanted to admit. "Since my feelings with her, I'm more in tune to how easily people fall into affairs. I'm more sensitive. I appreciate at a deeper level than I did before, because of my own attraction, how easy it would be to escape from the problems my wife and I were having."

Many pastors feel that they have never really been attracted sexually to a counselee or parishioner. Some have been in the pastoral ministry for many years without ever experiencing a strong attraction to a woman coming to them for help. A pastor may be well justified to conclude that he simply does not respond to women sexually in the counseling setting. When that is the case, it may be helpful for him and for his counselees to ponder some questions. How comfortable is he about his own sexuality? Does he leave his sexuality at home when he puts on a clerical collar and walks into his church office? Has he ever avoided counseling with certain women to whom he might be attracted? Has he maintained any illusions about never having any problems in this area out of a need to feel competent and on top of his counseling? Has he been blind to sexual issues raised by counselees that should have been dealt with directly? Or quite possibly has that right woman just not yet come to his office for his pastoral help? When she does come, will he be prepared to acknowledge his own humanity to himself when there is no question that he, too, has finally been turned on?

I like what is happening to me now, the fantasies, etc., and I'm holding on to it

In some instances a pastor recognizes right away that he is infatuated with a counselee, and he goes on for months and months never resolving his intense attraction for her. In such cases the pastor chooses to hold on to the fantasies and feelings, wanting to some extent the anguish of desiring a woman he knows he can't have. Perhaps this kind of situation is a safe sort of affair for a parish pastor. It brings him the personal satisfaction of wild sexual escapades in his daydreams, with the accompanying torment of being within arm's reach of the honeypot from which he will never have a taste. The pastor knows fully what is happening. He perpetuates the relationship by maintaining enough contact with the woman so she never says good-by. Probably his torment over the matter is necessary so that there is sufficient self-punishment for the good fantasies he is enjoying!

Pastor Jones asserts that he has "firmly faced up to the fact that I am sexually attracted to her," as he speaks of a parishioner who is active in his church. He really sees her only occasionally, the pastoral contacts being the informal type of brief visits to her home or short conversations when she stops by his office. Despite their infrequent contacts, Pastor Jones has entertained vivid fantasies about the woman.

> Well, she is not only vivacious and interested in what I am interested in, but she is a very good-looking woman. She's slender, trim, full of life. I find myself wondering sometimes just what it

would be like. With my wife I'm completely impotent.

Of course Pastor Jones has never revealed his secret feelings and fantasies either to the parishioner or to his wife. Rather, it is a private battle within himself, with enjoyment on one side and punishment on the other. The side that enjoys the fantasies tells him that his attraction to the woman proves he is not dead after all! But the guilty side never ceases to remind him, "Come on, fellow, this is against the moral law again."

Pastor Roberts frankly admits that he is enjoying his attraction to a counselee. At the same time he is not taking any definite steps to resolve his relationship with her or to resolve the matter of his own feelings within himself. He acknowledges to himself that he is attracted to the woman, but he feels in limbo, as if the situation is not completed. He has not told his wife, and of course he has not told the counselee. Fantasies usually lose most of their excitement when they are no longer one's private secret. As Pastor Roberts observed, he hasn't discussed his feelings with anybody else, probably because he likes the feelings, he enjoys them, and he isn't ready yet to let them go.

The woman is a fairly new member of Pastor Roberts' church, and she has come only twice for counseling about her marriage. He also sees her at community events and in the grocery store. She complains that her husband ignores her, and she gives Pastor Roberts the kind of look or attention that, he says, "clicks something within me." Once over the phone she seemed to say something to him that sounded like, "I love you," but it was said so quickly he could not be sure that was what she meant. But he certainly remembered it that way. He identified the factors accounting for his attraction to her: "The physical, and the feeling that here is a woman who seems to want me."

He has had sexual fantasies about her that he rarely has about any other women. But whatever enjoyment he has with his fantasies is accompanied by the disappointment that his daydreams are not to be fulfilled.

> It's a kind of alive feeling, a man-woman sort of thing. For me that's good. At the same time it's a frustrating feeling. It's like the cookie jar is there, but it's a no-no.

Moreover, his dilemma is compounded by his difficulty in treating her like any other parishioner. He says he finds himself avoiding her on routine calls because he is always questioning his motives for really wanting to see her. She has not been in church for quite awhile, and most any other parishioner would have been called on in such a case.

Many pastors can identify with situations like those told by Pastor Jones and Pastor Roberts. The fantasies are fun and safe, but they take up much time and energy, with an added degree of frustration. Sometimes it is helpful to a pastor simply to realize how he is tormenting himself by his choice to maintain this secret affair in his fantasies. He probably knows full well that if he were to share them with anyone else—particularly his wife—they would be shattered, and he would no longer have the bittersweet anguish of his secret love. Even if the pastor goes to another professional counselor or a colleague for help about the situation, he may say something about his dilemma but still choose to continue nurturing his fantasies without letting them go.

The pastor needs to ask himself why he wants to hold on to his feelings for the woman when he knows nothing will come of his relationship with her. Are his daydreams an escape from the problems of his church? Or does his infatuation with the counselee help divert his attention from the problems in his own marriage? Maybe the fantasies are his way of holding on to the counselee in order to increase his own sense of importance to her. If he really needs to be so important to the counselee, he may do well to explore that need farther to find out what it means about himself. And if he needs to have such a romanticized relationship with the counselee, he should ask himself whether he is trying to perpetuate her dependence on him so she never finds her own self-sufficiency.

Capitulation: This is what I've been waiting for

John Ordway has identified the situation in which a pastor decides that an intimate relationship with a particular woman is worth the sacrifice of his profession, his personal integrity, and his marriage.

> It is an IDEAL that he [the pastor] has long secretly hoped would show up; and when the woman offers herself as such an ideal, hoping for an ideal of manhood in return, his wildest hopes seem realized—judgment, duty, ministerial oath, wife, family, parochial obligations all go out the window. And he embraces his long-awaited true-lover—only to find with the passage of time that she is merely mortal—and a badly mixed-up one at that.[34]

The counselee may appear to be the ideal woman for the pastor, or the circumstances associated with the counselee may be the ideal. Not only may she be attractive physically and in terms of her personality, but the time spent with her may be ideal compared with the problems in the parish and in the parsonage, which the pastor prefers to try to forget. Whatever the woman and the circumstances represent to the pastor, he decides that what might be sacrificed will be well rewarded by the intimate relationship with the counselee. The early professional, pastor-parishioner contract soon changes after the pastor has decided that this woman really represents what he has been waiting for.

Pastor Snyder's ideal was an expressive, outgoing, and playful woman. He liked the playful mother quality about her and found that to be very sexy and very stimulating. He derived strength from her and found her acceptance of him as a person to be especially meaningful.

Pastor Snyder recognized his capitulation to the situation. Apparently he was willing to surrender so much because the woman represented what he had been waiting for over the years.

> I guess in one sense I felt justified on the basis of the fact that I had denied myself any kind of free expression of my feelings toward other women for so long, and so I felt that I had enough hurt and anger stamps collected over the years that I would be able to cash in with her over a long period of time.

And that he did.

If a pastor decides to capitulate to the opportunity to become the counselee's intimate friend or lover, he is then by choice giving up his function as pastor and counselor. He no longer has the goals that a counselor would normally have. His goal is now the working out of an interpersonal relationship that will somehow satisfy their mutual needs. However, even if a pastor is genuinely in love with a woman who was initially a counselee, at least out of concern for her well-being he should ask himself if he has in any way taken advantage of her emotional vulnerability when she came for counseling. If that be the case, he has probably compounded her problems while using her need for help as the occasion to divert his attention from his own problems. Several years later Pastor Snyder was able to look back and see how his relationship with the counselee had not been helpful to either of them.

> In my somber moments of serious reflection I knew our relationship was simply keeping her from facing her poor marriage. And for me it became a crutch so I didn't have to make any self-discovery about who I am, my powers, and my person. It didn't bring me ultimate fulfillment.

I'm helpless: what do I do now?

A pastoral counselor may find himself confronted with a sexually stimulating woman and be sure of only two things: He feels terribly uncomfortable about his aroused feelings, and he doesn't know what to do about the situation. Consequently, the pastor may experience sheer panic. Can he at least hope to endure his discomfort till the session ends and he or the woman departs? In any event, the counselor has dealt with himself by becoming helpless, not choosing any viable alternative for coping.

Pastor Wrigley had just such a situation occur when he was talking with a sixteen-year-old girl in his church. According to the pastor the girl had an attractive figure and an equally attractive face and eyes. Moreover, she seemed to have quite a suggestive walk, and she wore short dresses and a low blouse or a tight sweater.

During one particular conversation between Pastor Wrigley and the girl the pastor felt total panic the whole twenty minutes the conversation lasted. While they were talking, he was acutely aware of her and felt very uncomfortable.

> Her smile is almost like she is coming in on me. She can be ten feet away, but she really zeroes in on the face contact. The thing that goes through my mind is that if there is one girl that wants to get laid it is this girl.

He explained what he was afraid of: "She might say, 'Let's go out back and lay each other.' " He just tried to cover his panic and his anxiety the best he could, though he recalled that he really did not try to do anything about the situation. "I acted helpless," he acknowledged, instead of doing something either to end the conversation or to ease his own personal discomfort.

In a different case, Pastor Norris felt much less anxiety, but he definitely felt ill at ease as he talked with the counselee. He could tell that his sexual feelings were making him "sloppy around the edges" as a counselor. He described the woman, who is just a few years younger than he, quite simply: "She's beautiful. I like her style. I like the way she handles herself in the different situations I've seen." He arranged the seating so he would not have to look at her legs. Nonetheless, as she talked about her affair with a married man, and as she wondered what others in the church would think, the pastor was increasingly aware of his personal discomfort and embarrassment. He clearly felt "directionless" about what to do with the interview.

Because of his confusion, he tried unsuccessfully to

ask several clarifying questions throughout the interview, but his embarrassment persisted. He felt quite frustrated because his attraction to the woman was intruding, he was certain, upon the counseling process. The session ended, the pastor felt, with a sense of "fleeing" from the situation on the part of each of them. He wished he could have handled it differently: "I don't have the skill or training to make fruitful use of my own feelings, though I suspect one could have."

The counselor who finds himself in a panic and feeling quite helpless about his overwhelming feelings of attraction may take some comfort in knowing there is nothing peculiar about his plight. Not only most men, but probably also most ministers, can identify with that kind of personal dilemma. If, however, a counselor is frequently panic-stricken when relating to attractive women, he may find it useful to explore the matter through psychotherapy. There may be some significant reasons why he repeatedly chooses to be helpless or impotent when a woman comes to him for help.

Lord, help me with this

Encountering feelings and professional situations that are to some degree threatening, the pastor may naturally make the matter a subject for personal prayer. Pastor Swenson recalled three instances in his ministry in which he was strongly attracted to counselees. In one situation a young woman talked with him about baptism by immersion, and the pastor had vivid fantasies of being able to touch her during the baptismal service. The second situation involved a teen-age girl who confronted Pastor Swenson with her belief that he, like others in the church, would like to have sex with her. He did not tell her she was correct. And in the third instance he was counseling the wife of one of his closest personal friends. In that pastoral relationship his sexual attraction was mixed with friendship, Christian love, and a lot of just plain concern for her.

On all three occasions Pastor Swenson was extremely concerned about his feelings and what they meant. Out of his concern he prayed that God would either remove his feelings of attraction or at least help him to overcome them and relate to the counselees in ways that would be helpful to them. The pastor believes these personal struggles were positive because they deepened his prayer life as he relied on spiritual resources to help him cope with his feelings toward the three women.

Prayer is an important personal resource for the pastoral counselor. It is natural and appropriate for a pastor to make problems he is experiencing with his counselees an object of serious prayer. Moreover, the counselor may, to his benefit, examine how he uses prayer when dealing with his own sexuality. On the one hand, the pastor may be inviting additional problems if his prayers become a means for either denying or avoiding the impact of his sexual feelings upon the counseling relationship. If, on the other hand, prayer helps him to be more honest and candid with himself about his sexual feelings, he will more likely handle the issue in a constructive way.

Shall I handle this myself or seek help?

When dealing with himself a pastor attracted to a counselee will make a choice about whether to discuss the situation with another professional person. An increasing number of pastors are utilizing a variety of opportunities for obtaining consultation about their

counseling. Some men go to a fellow pastor. More ministers are meeting in small support groups in which they
can discuss their feelings candidly. The use of such resources should become more common as pastors realize
the benefits of receiving feedback and support from
their colleagues.

Often many pastors feel that the counseling situation
is not extraordinary enough or disturbing enough to
merit outside consultation. Their choice is to handle
their sexual feelings themselves. One pastor explained:
"I don't really feel it's [his sexual attraction] unique, at
least for me; it's not a burden I carry or anything."
Another minister simply explained he hadn't sought
consultation because his attraction to the counselee
"wasn't important."

A crucial issue for any pastor as he decides whether
to seek another's opinion is whether matters discussed
in confidence remain confidential. Two pastors emphasized how this was a critical concern for them. The first
had no one he could talk with. "There isn't a person
within immediate touch here right now with whom I
would share this counseling situation. I'm a very lonely
person."

And the other minister spoke not only of his isolation
from persons he can trust but also of how such isolation
may lead him to worry that his feelings of sexual attraction may be abnormal.

> I'd say right now I'm pretty isolated. I don't know
> if I would want to take the risk of bringing this
> up as a topic for a group session or in a group of
> friends. There might be one or two people that
> I might venture forth with if it becomes an over-
> riding kind of thing, but I'm not ready to take the
> first step in a group of other ministers. I would

say my feelings are that this attraction is more normal than abnormal, but maybe, if I dwell on one situation, I might start thinking, Well, maybe this is abnormal. If I think it is abnormal, it makes me uncomfortable.

The importance of outside consultation for a pastor's counseling cannot be overstressed. Such consultation is not an indication of incompetence. Quite the contrary, it is a mark of professional discipline to allow one's work to be examined by another professional person. When a pastor is attracted to a female counselee, he may rightly conclude that the matter is of little consequence to him or the counselee and that he can handle it comfortably. However, he should always ask himself if his failure to check it out with a professional reflects either an anxious need to cover up, or a desire to continue a situation for questionable reasons.

She has the problem, not me

A pastor may deal with his own anxieties by blaming the counselee for what he feels. Pastor Forbes was aware, upon later reflection, that that was indeed what he had done. The situation involved a woman who was a member of his church but whom he did not know very well. The young woman had never married, and had often been in trouble because of her illicit sexual activities. She came to the pastor's office to talk about her problem, which was promiscuous sexual activity.

Listening to the recital of the woman's sexual behavior soon became an arousing experience for Pastor Forbes. The story she told was really fascinating because of its scandalous character. The woman had been sexually involved with a number of prominent persons in the community whom the minister knew.

He described his experience listening to her story: "It was like reading a dirty book, that kind of experience. The story was intriguing. In terms of my own feelings, I was sexually aroused." Also, he was more interested in the details of her story than he was in her as a person. "I think I realized as I listened to her that I wasn't relating to her as a person. I was interested in her story. I was letting her tell her story and almost using her in that sense."

Pastor Forbes's response in the counseling session was to give the woman what he regarded as good advice, an exhortation to change her ways and live a more respectable life. As he later discussed his response to the woman, he recognized that his demand for the woman to change could well have been for the benefit of his own anxieties.

> You know, when you think about it, it might well be that my exhortation to her might have solved a lot of problems for myself. I was sort of slapping her on the wrists for doing awful things that I liked to hear about.

Pastor Forbes had shifted the responsibility for his discomfort to the counselee. Yes, in a remote fashion it could be suggested that if the woman had not led a promiscuous life, the counselor would not have been sexually aroused. It would be about as relevant to say that if she had not even come to see him, he would not have been aroused either. But such reasoning is pointless. The fundamental issue is that the woman's promiscuity was symptomatic that she was a deeply distressed person seeking help. The counselor chose to respond to her by blaming her for his aroused feelings.

The counselee is responsible for her life but not for the counselor's sexual arousal. The counselor could have chosen numerous other responses such as concern, pity, anger, or, better yet, patient caring for a troubled person. When a counselor has not clarified for himself that he is responsible for his own emotional reactions, there is the real likelihood he will put that burden on the counselee. Obviously the counselee has sufficient difficulty, whatever the personal crisis that brings her to counseling, in taking responsibility for herself without having to take responsibility for the counselor's feelings as well.

I am comfortable with my sexual feelings

Pastors have also reported occasions with counselees when they have dealt with themselves by being comfortable with their own sexual feelings. Pastor Reynolds has told about a woman to whom he was attracted who was a close friend of a terminally ill parishioner. His relationship with the woman centered mainly around the approaching death of the friend. He spoke of the woman as being warm and open, which accounted largely for his attraction to her. "I was conscious that I was always glad to see her for any given reason and would go with a different feeling than if it were someone who was not so attractive."

Pastor Reynolds allowed himself to enjoy his attraction to the woman without any guilt or chagrin about his feelings. This was permissible for him because of his personal decision that his feelings were never to be acted on.

> The desire to hold her was probably there. Once when she held my arm and pulled it, more than likely by accident, against her body, it was a pleasurable experience for me. You don't take advantage of those things, nor need to have any desire to follow up an advantage in order to make it a pleasant experience.

He noted also that the pleasant feelings he enjoyed when he was with her probably prompted him to find other occasions to be with her.

> I think I tried to evaluate what I was feeling in this kind of experience and to put it in the normal perspectives of a pastoral ministry. Also to keep in mind the human dimension of it. I saw nothing wrong with the feeling I had within myself, and had no desire to pursue it any farther. But without a doubt I probably manufactured two or three more times to see her than I otherwise would have. I decided that a man does not cut off the pleasure of another woman's company just because he is married and his relationship to his wife is secure and happy. I decided that as long as nothing untoward occurred, either internal or external, then why not enjoy the experience or why shut it off because it happens?

For Pastor Todman, however, there had been a time earlier in his ministry when he found his sexual feelings for counselees to be quite distressing. But as the years went by he became more comfortable with those feelings. So when Betty Stewart came for counsel he dealt with himself by accepting his sexual response to her. He felt comfortable about his feelings, knowing that they would not be acted out and also knowing that he had a secure relationship with his wife.

> To me Betty Stewart was a very attractive person in all respects. She was charming, intellectual, physically beautiful. While she certainly attracted me in every department, I didn't feel threatened by the attraction. I was saying to myself, Well, any healthy male is going to be at-

tracted by such a good looking gal who is also personable, has intellectual attributes, and everything else. I just simply said, O.K., sure I'm attracted. I never felt it would get out of hand or anything of that nature.

Each of the several cases that have been outlined was chosen to illustrate some of the typical responses of pastors toward themselves when they are sexually aroused with a counselee. These examples do not exhaust the full range of possibilities, but they do indicate general patterns of ministers' experiences. Several different responses could occur while working with the same counselee. A pastor might at first experience anxiety or ambivalence about his initial attraction and later reach a point of acceptance and genuine comfort with himself about his feelings. The main purpose in discussing these various cases is so that pastors may recognize more easily the kinds of options they may choose when they are attracted to a counselee.

ESSENTIALS FOR THE COUNSELOR TO COPE EFFECTIVELY WITH HIMSELF

Effective coping with one's own sexual feelings in a counseling relationship requires honest awareness of one's feelings and behavior. The pastor is inviting potential difficulties for the counselee as well as for himself if he is blind to the depths and dimensions of his own sexual reactions. E. Mansell Pattison, a psychiatrist, has commented on this important point.

> The most difficult task to learn in psychotherapy is how to handle one's own reactions to the emotional currents of intense interpersonal relation-

ships. The same problem is no less true for the pastor, particularly because he is socially and emotionally much more intimately involved with the people with whom he works.

The pastor who is afraid of his own sexuality may deny his erotic feelings in situations where he should be aware that he is responding in a sexually provocative or reactive fashion. Often pastors find women accusing them of improper advances while the pastor protests his innocence. Had the pastor recognized his own impulses he might have avoided playing into a mutual sexual distortion of the relationship.[35]

If sexuality in counseling is to be handled professionally and with pastoral care and insight, the place to begin is with the counselor himself and his personal response to his own feelings. Besides his personal reflection on his responses to counselees, he can be greatly aided in this process if he will find a trusted colleague or an experienced fellow counselor with whom he feels comfortable discussing his sexuality.

Another essential point for coping effectively is for the pastor to take full responsibility for his emotional responses to counselees. Theological clarity requires the pastor to assume that kind of responsibility for himself. No set of circumstances precludes the basic nature of man as a choice maker. We are free to respond; and so radical is that freedom that we are even responsible, as Christians, for those dimensions of ourselves over which we seem to have little or no control. The views, "She seduced me," or, "She's so sexually aggressive I was helpless," are thinly veiled excuses for abdicating personal responsibility. If indeed the counselor wants to believe he is helpless, then he will allow himself to be sexually manipulated instead of coping to the benefit of the counselee and himself.

A vital consequence of a counselor's claiming responsibility for his own sexual responses is that the burden of his feelings is not placed on the counselee. This distinction has critical therapeutic significance. A counselee is responsible for herself and for being true to herself insofar as she knows herself. She is not responsible for a counselor's response to her when she is genuinely being herself. Her goal is to learn to be a responsible person who happens also to be a female. If she is told she is responsible for the reactions of the counselor or men in general, there is less likelihood she will develop a clear sense of her own personal identity, particularly as a sexual being.

The pastor who is able to deal more comfortably with his own sexuality becomes more trusting of those feelings in the counseling process. Trusting his sexual responses, the pastor will come to regard his feelings as a significant dimension of the counseling process and not as an annoying or inappropriate intrusion. The experienced counselor knows that all his feelings give him important data that can be used beneficially for the counselee.

For example, if the pastor is sexually attracted to the woman, that may well mean that other significant persons in her life are also similarly attracted to her, with important implications for her. Moreover, the pastor's feelings may give him clues about how the woman uses her sexuality. Is she comfortable with it? Is her sexuality an integrated dimension of her personality and interpersonal functioning? Or does the counselor indeed feel seduced, manipulated, or kept off guard? If that is the case, the counselor's goal may be to help the woman see how she uses her sexuality to hide her deep sense of inadequacy. The counselor can do this only when he trusts that his feelings are very appropriate to the counseling process and when he can help the woman to examine her own behavior without having to take responsibility for his feelings.

Finally, to achieve a more accepting response to his own sexuality a pastor may wish to consider the benefits of investing in psychotherapy for himself. A more honest look at one's self could be an excellent means for a pastor to integrate more fully his theology with his personal humanity. If that integration were indeed to occur, there could be quite positive benefits for his counselees!

4
The Pastor Deals
with the Counselee

> The minister's essential humanity is one of the precious things he has to share in all his relationships. If he puts on a "counseling approach," of whatever kind, he confuses his counselees by the mask which obscures his personhood.—Howard J. Clinebell, Jr.[36]

MARIA'S HANDS pulled nervously on the shredded tissue. The tears wetting her cheeks accompanied the desperate tone in her voice. This was not the first time she had talked of suicide to Pastor Barns. While Maria told of her despairing outlook, Pastor Barns was reviewing vivid memory flashes of being awakened six weeks earlier at 2:30 A.M. with a call from the hospital. Maria's husband, Tom, was calling to say that she had overdosed with sleeping tablets for the third time. Once again the angry frustration and overpowering hopelessness so evident in everything Maria said stirred an uneasy premonition in Pastor Barns. She would soon try again what she had failed at six weeks before.

Pastor Barns had been trying to help Maria for more than half a year. She was at least fifteen years younger than he, and though Pastor Barns was nearing fifty, he still responded with sexual feelings to this pretty woman. Maria was from the lower socioeconomic level. She was always struggling to get a little more money from the state or from the last man she lived with. In spite of the depression that hung like a pall over Maria's demeanor, there was a clear beauty about her simple features. More than once it had occurred to Pastor Barns that if Maria could somehow get on top of her problems, and if she could find a man who wouldn't cause her so much grief, she could be a beautiful woman. He knew that he not only felt affection for Maria but that he was genuinely attracted to her. His heart went out to her as she sat weeping; how could someone so gentle and fair be so near to destroying her own life?

Elsewhere another parish pastor faced a quite different professional dilemma. When Pastor Doyle came to First Church five years ago, Alice was one of the first persons he met. She was aggressive about introducing herself, and the pastor soon realized he found her to be quite attractive and pleasant to be with. Nearly his own age, the pastor said of her, she "is short of stature and she has a nice figure. She dresses stylishly—I think sexy. She has a sexy voice, sort of soft. She comes on at times helpless, like a little girl who needs to be protected, and that kind of gets to me."

Pastor Doyle sees Alice in many of the programs and activities of the church. She is on his governing board, and they often work together on church projects. Recently, Alice had sensed that Pastor Doyle was acting strangely around her. He seemed cool toward her and less friendly. This bothered her as she thought about it, so she called him for an appointment in his office. When she arrived for the meeting, she came directly to the point and told Pastor Doyle she felt there was some kind of problem getting in the way of their relationship.

As soon as the words were out of Alice's mouth, Pastor

Doyle's mind began spinning. He felt his blood pressure starting to mount. He knew he had been uncomfortable in Alice's presence lately, because he had been having vivid sexual feelings and fantasies about her. They made him feel uncomfortable in relating to her. He didn't know what to do. He really felt trapped by her bluntness in raising the issue so directly. Frantic questions raced through his mind: Do I, a minister, tell a parishioner how I really feel about her? Is that the wisest thing? I don't want this to get out. I don't want my wife to know. I'm trapped, and I think Alice knows it!

Those two pastors were having to decide how to handle their own feelings of attraction to a counselee in a way that would serve the best interests of the woman while not jeopardizing their own professional integrity. For Pastor Barns the woman was suicidal and clearly in the midst of another personal crisis that threatened to drive her to another suicide attempt. Pastor Doyle, on the other hand, was faced with a parishioner who simply wanted to know why her five-year relationship with her pastor had broken down. What must these two pastors and other pastors in similar situations consider if each is to help a woman with her problems and at the same time protect his own interests as a pastor of a church and a leader in the community?

GUIDELINES FOR THE PASTOR

How does the pastoral counselor best help the counselee? That is the basic question at all times for a pastor, and it remains the primary question when the counselor is attracted to her. Unfortunately for both pastors and their counselees, in the past many pastors were warned to steer clear of sexual issues when counseling women. And if such issues couldn't be avoided, then the pastor had better first of all seek to protect himself. This is really an abdication of pastoral responsibility. The pastor's first consideration is to decide what he can do as a counselor that will be in the woman's best interests in helping her deal with her problems.

This is not to say that the pastor forgets that he has a reputation to maintain. This is a realistic concern for the parish pastor, and will enter at some point into every situation a minister encounters where his own sexuality is involved. Stroup and Wood have correctly observed that there is a deep-rooted cultural expectation that ministers should be asexual, as though there may be something more godly about being a eunuch.[37] But if that myth has survived too long in the church, it may be in part because pastors in too many cases have been too willing to let it go unchallenged. As a pastor achieves increasing maturity in dealing with his own sexuality, including his sexual responses to a variety of persons, he may find it easier to assume the risk involved when he lets his humanity be known.

The value framework discussed in Chapter 2 is my way of saying what I believe is the best way for a pastor to help any counselee. The counseling relationship is essentially dialogical, a communication of being with being to the end that the counselee may find new resources and insight for living. Within that process it is fundamental that the counselor's humanness be apparent without being intrusive. This is necessary for clarifying lines of responsibility, which is to say each person is responsible for his own feelings. My working assumption throughout is that mental and spiritual well-being requires seeing oneself emotionally as a free responder to his environment and not as the helpless victim of persons and circumstances. Furthermore, as in all relationships, there must be a beginning and an end, a time to say hello and a time to say good-by. Effective helping relationships have clear limits. This perspective offers a pastor several specific points to examine when deciding what is best for him to do for a counselee to whom he is attracted.

1. *The pastor must assess the dynamics occurring between him and the counselee.* He needs to determine as best he can the causes for his sexual response to the woman.

His self-questioning may run in this vein: Would this woman be attractive to me in any setting? Is she the type of woman I have been drawn to over the years? What is happening in the counseling session that may be intensifying my response to her? Have we been talking about sexual topics, her lovelife, or marital problems of a sexual nature? Does the woman seem passive and dependent, so I am giving her a lot of support? Do I like being her source of strength? Does this woman strike me as sexually promiscuous? Is she seeming to show off her charms to me as an invitation?

As a pastor ponders these questions he can understand better the nature of his sexual response. For example, he may decide that the woman under any other circumstances wouldn't attract his attention, but she has had affairs with four men and seems available to anyone. It may not be her beauty that attracts, but her apparent availability.

Likewise, if it is her dependency a pastor likes, he may decide her demands for his support aren't so attractive as he first felt. Or a pastor may realize it was the discussion of sexual matters that was arousing his sexual interest more than any features about the woman herself.

This initial assessment is necessary so a pastor can

determine the nature and extent of his sexual interest. After giving it some reflection a pastor may find his sexual attraction is less a problem than he had believed.

2. *The pastor determines for himself the relative intensity of his actual sexual attraction to the woman.* If a pastor is willing to be aware of himself, he may have several personal clues to the strength of his attraction to the counselee. During the counseling session he may be aware of a casual interest in the woman's personality or her physical features, or he may have some brief sexual fantasies about the woman. More obvious clues to sexual attraction are evident if the pastor experiences anxiety or nervousness, difficulty in speaking, fantasies interrupting his concentration, and trouble focusing the direction of the interview. Outside the counseling hour the pastor may have thoughts and fantasies, perhaps even dreams about the woman, clearly pointing up his attraction to her.

The pastor should also be aware of any deviation in his counseling style when working with the woman. If he finds significant changes from his normal behavior, such as overpoliteness, reluctance to disappoint, or difficulty in asking confronting questions, these may be indications that he is more attracted to her than he at first wanted to acknowledge.

By consciously checking the degree of his attraction, the counselor decreases the possibility that he may unknowingly play sex games with her. The sexual dimension to the counseling relationship thus becomes a matter of increased conscious surveillance. Then the pastor will be in a better position to decide how his sexual feelings are affecting the counseling process.

Some pastors may mistakenly assume that if they control or "hide" their sexual discomfort, their feelings are not having any impact on the counseling process. This false notion invites serious problems. If a pastor is attracted in any degree, his feelings will most likely have some kind of direct influence upon the counseling relationship. This cannot be emphasized too strongly! Choosing to remain unaware of those feelings, or dismissing them as trivial or insignificant, is to do a professional disservice to the woman and to the counselor himself. One experienced pastor was both candid and wise when he said about himself: "I'll admit that women counselees who are attractive to me get more attention than those who are not attractive to me."

3. *The pastor decides whether or not it is appropriate to refer to himself and what he is experiencing in the counseling interview.* This kind of decision would include references not just to the counselor's sexual feelings but also to any other personal feelings he may have, including anger, tiredness, happiness, and sadness. It is important for the counselee to be aware of the counselor's human qualities, but the counselor has to judge the appropriate times for such disclosures.

Generally speaking, crisis counseling should preclude any personal references to the counselor. Here we are speaking of the kind of personal crisis that has recently and traumatically disrupted the counselee's pattern of living. A death in the immediate family is an obvious example. Likewise losing one's job, breaking off an engagement to be married, or failing in school. In these kinds of life situations the counselee is faced with the critical necessity of solving an immediate problem so stability may be restored to her life. The pastor in this type of situation best helps the counselee by focusing on the immediate problem, helping the counselee sort out the confusion, and identifying practical alternatives for action. The pastor then challenges the counselee to cope by choosing a course of action to follow.[38] Throughout this process the counselee's energies and resources must be directed totally to the problem to be solved. It would only be distracting for the pastor to interject anything more than the briefest personal references to himself and any of his own feelings.

Much of the counseling pastors are required to do is crisis counseling. But certainly not all of it is a responding to alarms and a calming of emergencies. Many persons have problems that are not of recent origin but, rather, have a long history. So the pastor deals with ongoing marital problems, personality disorders related to incidents in one's childhood, as well as counseling for personal growth, which involves a consideration of the totality of one's life. These are not crisis situations if the counselee is functioning fairly well on a daily basis and doesn't feel her basic pattern of life is seriously threatened. In such cases the pastor may consider the appropriateness of references to himself, including the reporting of his sexual response to the counselee.

In the cases that opened this chapter, it would certainly have been a distraction to Maria, on the verge of suicide, for Pastor Barns to tell her he is attracted to her. Maria needed to concentrate all her attention on dealing with the problems overwhelming her at the moment. By contrast, Alice was not in any personal emergency when she came to see Pastor Doyle. Alice was coping well with her daily life and, while concerned, was not upset or distraught about the apparent breakdown in her relationship with her minister. She came simply to see if Pastor Doyle could help to clarify her relationship with him. In such a situation, references to himself were appropriate, and Pastor Doyle decided to level with Alice about his feelings toward her. Alice replied that she had thought he felt that way and that she was glad they could talk honestly about it and get it cleared up.

4. *The pastor will make a decision about how vulnerable he wants to be regarding his professional reputation.* What are the risks in telling this particular counselee he is attracted to her? Will she understand what he is saying, or will she regard his feelings as an invitation to go to bed? Will she be offended and feel that the pastor has behaved unprofessionally? Will she report the matter to others in the congregation? What is the possibility that ill-founded rumors will fly through the community? What kinds of stories will get back to the pastor's wife?

Pastor Schmidt makes it a regular practice to talk with each of the high school students about their future life goals. The interviews last about thirty minutes in his study at the church. Susan had been active through the years in the church youth program. Now eighteen, she was thinking about her plans for college and possible marriage. While talking with Susan, Pastor Schmidt was disturbed by the strength of his attraction to her. Not only was he attracted to her personality and her flirtatious mannerisms, but he was also drawn to her striking young figure. As she described the different colleges she was considering, the pastor caught himself fantasizing about undressing her. He was having a difficult time really listening to what she was saying.

Afterward Pastor Schmidt said that he could never have told her what was occurring to him, or that he was even attracted to her. "From a personal or a professional standpoint I felt that it would not be beneficial to share my feelings with her. If I had told her, I'm sure she would have told others, and I could forget my job!"

Probably in many counseling situations there will be some element of risk of being misunderstood if a pastor is frank about his sexual feelings. But a pastor will be in less of a bind in dealing with this question if he does not have an unspoken agreement with his church that he must at all times appear to be asexual. The pastor who conveys to his parishioners that he is not endowed with the full range of human experiences and feelings—including the sexual—will be threatened by any possibility that news to the contrary gets out. If, on the other hand, a pastor is comfortable with his sexuality as a normal part of his equipment as a human being, he may be able to evaluate more reasonably the extent to which he really is taking a risk in acknowledging his attraction to a counselee.

5. *The pastor must decide if he is prepared to define the counseling as a professional relationship within certain specific limits verbally stated to the counselee.* This question is finally decided in the pastor's own mind and heart. Whatever form his thoughts may take, it must boil down to something like this: Regardless of how strongly attracted I am to her, I am professionally her pastor, and I will keep this counseling relationship within necessary limits so the counseling benefits her primarily.

This decision is necessary regardless of how close he and the woman may be as friends on other occasions. In choosing him as her confidante, pastor, and counselor, she approaches him as more than a friend. She approaches him as one having certain training and skills that will help her deal with a personal dilemma. Pastoral counseling is always a professional relationship, and as a professional relationship there will generally be some verbal limits.

Limits may take a variety of forms. The use of time can be a very important limitation. "We shall have fifty-minute appointments, beginning at 4:00 P.M. and ending shortly before 5:00." If the counselee arrives twenty-five minutes late, the pastor may adhere to the five o'clock ending time to demonstrate that their use of time formally defines their relationship. One pastor observes the time limitation by having his secretary buzz on the intercom when the fifty minutes is up. The buzz is a signal that the session must draw to a close. Just a simple, "It is time for us to stop today," or, "We must end in a few minutes," is an unobtrusive but clear way to observe the time limit.

There can be other important limitations. A pastor may put a firm limit on the kind of touching to occur between him and the counselee during sessions. Excessive hugging or touching when the two are alone may confuse the counselee about the professional nature of the relationship.

A pastor may also decide to put some limit on the number and nature of their conversations. He may state such a limit in this manner: "I believe the best way for me to help you is with weekly sessions in my office. You may certainly call me on the phone if you feel a need to. However, I generally feel that long conversations on the phone are not helpful. I would prefer that we deal in depth with your concerns during the sessions on Wednesday."

Many pastors say they are reluctant either to set any limits at all on pastoral services to their parishioners, or, if they do observe limits, to make them verbally explicit. When dealing with sexual matters, however, a pastor is unduly careless if he is unwilling to state the limits of the relationship. It should be verbally clear to both the pastor and the parishioner that regardless of what sexual material they discuss or what feelings either of them experiences, the professional limits to the relationship will not be altered. Sessions will not run forty-five minutes overtime, limits about touching will be observed, long and frequent phone calls will be discouraged, and appointments will not be scheduled at more frequent intervals.

The problem of setting limits came up for Pastor Hartz when he encountered a situation familiar to many counselors. It happened when Ed and Sylvia, members of his congregation, were going through a rocky time in their marriage. Besides being parishioners, Ed and Sylvia had also become close friends with Pastor Hartz and his wife, Helen. This friendship, valued by both couples, threatened to confuse matters for the pastor when he had to put on his professional hat.

Hartz attributed part of his discomfort to the fact that Sylvia had a rather relaxed attitude toward sexual relations outside of marriage. Her rather free life-style held some attraction for the pastor, who came from a more traditional background. Moreover, he found Sylvia's physical features and style of dress to be especially attractive. Pastor Hartz described the problem this way:

> So when she was under strain or stress, and she would break down and cry, there was the tendency on her part to want to have some kind of physical contact for comfort or support. It was difficult to maintain a professional relationship while I was very much aware that this person was more than a counseling client. She was a friend. Moreover, I had this intense awareness of her womanness.

Pastor Hartz had to set limits as a counselor right from the start. His first counseling session with Sylvia was in her home when her husband, Ed, was away. After he sat down on the couch Sylvia sat down beside him, which on various social occasions she had often done. As they talked about the bitterness between Sylvia and Ed, she became increasingly upset. It was clear to Pastor Hartz that Sylvia wanted a physical expression from him of support and comfort. It was then that he told her that if he was to be of any help to her they could not be sitting together on the couch. He moved over to another chair and arranged with her for their subsequent sessions to be at his office. On other occasions as couples Pastor Hartz and Sylvia had hugged each other as an appropriate demonstration of their affection for one another as friends. But as a pastor Hartz had to be definitive with Sylvia about the limits of the counseling relationship. Otherwise he could not have dealt with the sexual dynamics he, for one, was aware of in their relationship.

6. *Finally, the pastor must make a judgment as to whether there will likely be a positive benefit for the counselee if he reports to her his attraction.* This decision assumes that the answers to the first five questions have been positive. "Yes, I am aware of feelings of sexual attraction in this counseling session." "Yes, these feelings are intense enough to have a bearing on the counseling situation." "Yes, this is not crisis counseling and any personal reference to me will not distract the counselee from dealing with an emergency life problem." "Yes, I am prepared to accept the risk of letting this person know that I have sexual feelings, even toward her." "Yes, I am prepared verbally to set limits that will define my relationship with this woman as a

professional counseling relationship." In the framework of these positive responses, the pastor may see several possible benefits for the woman.

—There can be a positive benefit if the pastor's honesty about his sexual feelings is a genuine communication of his humanness. A counselee is not helped if the pastor hides his humanity and his masculinity behind a mask of asexual religiosity. The counselee may find it much easier to affirm and accept her own humanness as she experiences the pastor affirming his.

—Another positive benefit may be the deepening of the level of honesty between counselee and counselor. A counselee may have some anxiety about being rejected if the pastor should really know the truth about her. But when the pastor demonstrates his own openness about himself, he shows he can also be accepting of a similar level of vulnerability in the counselee.

—There may be another benefit for the woman if the sexual dynamics between her and the pastor have in some way been blocking the counseling process. We know that in every heterosexual relationship there are at least some sexual dynamics occurring, even if they are not readily apparent on the surface. An innocent sexual enjoyment of each other may produce a casualness between a pastor and a female counselee that precludes any serious counseling. Subtle flirting by both persons may make it impossible for the pastor to be even slightly confronting where confrontation would ordinarily be appropriate. A candid discussion by a pastor and counselee of their attraction to each other may help to undercut the flirting games so the counseling can move beyond those games to the deeper issues troubling the counselee.

—If a woman uses her sexuality to manipulate others,

the counselor will probably respond to this ploy with his own feelings of attraction. The revelation of his sexual feelings may beneficially be used as a "here and now" exhibit of how the woman is relating to him. Although the woman is not responsible for the counselor's feelings, it may be beneficial for her to recognize the behavior on her part to which the pastor is responding. This learning could be especially useful for the counselee if she uses her sexual behavior as a mask to hide some insecurity in herself that she does not want others to see.

—It can also be a benefit to the woman if the pastor reports his sexual attraction in the context of a general understanding that he owns his feelings totally as his own response to her. The pastor may make this clear by saying that he alone is responsible for how he feels. This does not mean he switches his feelings off and on at will, but more significantly it means that he accepts responsibility for how he feels without blaming her for his feeling responses to her. In this way the counselee may learn from the counselor's example that she likewise is responsible for her feelings, sexual as well as others. Her feelings are her own responses, and this new attitude can free her from viewing herself as just a pawn of circumstances. She can discover herself as a free responder to whatever situation she confronts.

—Finally, by being able to talk about his own sexual responses the pastor demonstrates that he is not afraid of sexuality, either his own or the counselee's. This may greatly assist the counselee in being more willing to explore the meaning of her own sexuality if that is an important life issue for her.

If the pastor decides to raise the issue of his attraction to the counselee, he might do it in the following manner:

PASTOR: I'm aware that I feel attracted to you. I think it is important for me to be clear about this because my feelings may be affecting what has been happening in this session.

COUNSELEE: I hadn't been aware of anything. But I can say I've been attracted to you at different times too.

PASTOR: I want you to know that any feelings I may have about you won't change my relationship to you as a pastor and counselor. I won't do anything more about my feelings than report them.

COUNSELEE: Well, I guess that's what we're here for—to talk about feelings. I appreciate your honesty. Actually sex, I mean my feelings about sex, is hard for me to talk about with anyone.

PASTOR: You seem to have some pretty strong feelings about sex.

COUNSELEE: Yes. Well, it is kind of embarrassing. I would like to get into that sometime.

PASTOR: I would like us to explore anything that may be important for you. I want you to know that you are not responsible for any feelings I may have. I take full responsibility for whatever I feel in these sessions.

COUNSELEE: O.K. In that case I feel a little freer about leveling about some of my sexual feelings.

PASTOR: Do you want to say more?

COUNSELEE: Well, I've had problems relating to men for quite a few years. They think I'm leading them on and I'm not meaning to. They get mad at me. I flirt with men but I never let myself have an honest relationship with them. It creates a lot of problems in my work and with my husband.

PASTOR: And maybe some of that was happening here with me.

COUNSELEE: Probably. I was scared to come to see you.

But I knew that for this counseling to help I would have to be honest with you, and that's been hard for me in the past.

PASTOR: So you had some serious reservations about talking with me.

COUNSELEE: Yes. But you've been honest about some of your feelings. I don't think you'll take advantage of me. I think I can trust you.

PASTOR: Does what we're talking about now relate to some of the problems with your husband you mentioned at the beginning?

COUNSELEE: Well, yes, they do, as a matter of fact. He's very jealous, and treats me like a little girl all the time. I feel like he has a leash on me.

PASTOR: Go on.

The purpose of this verbatim account is to demonstrate how a counseling interview might move when a pastor reveals his attraction to the counselee. The pastor defines the context in which he reports his feelings, namely, that they may be important data but they don't change the counseling relationship. The woman says this is a subject that is not only difficult for her to talk about but that it has been a problem for her in various interpersonal relationships. The pastor's willingness to be honest about his own feelings facilitates her being less anxious about her feelings. The pastor clarifies his responsibility for his own feelings and brings the focus of the interview back to the problems the counselee is dealing with. At the end there is the clear indication that her sexuality is directly related to her troubled marriage and a domineering husband. By reporting his feelings in a professional manner the pastor has facilitated the woman's work on her present problems.

KEEPING SIGHT OF THE PURPOSE

The purpose for the pastor in reporting his sexual feelings is principally to deal openly with sexual dynamics that may be influencing or blocking the counseling process in such a way that the counselee is not getting all the help she needs. *If that purpose is lost sight of, then the reporting of the pastor's sexual response may become counterproductive for the counselee.* This may occur if the discussion of each other's sexual response becomes the chief purpose of the counseling instead of simply a means for moving ahead on other issues in the counselee's life. The crux of this problem is illustrated by Pastor Mainer's experience with Cherie.

Cherie was a very pretty woman and about the same age as Pastor Mainer. She was a Sunday school teacher, and Pastor Mainer had always been attracted by her physical appearance, more so than by her personality. There were the usual occasions at various meetings when he saw Cherie, including church meetings held in her home. He privately enjoyed her beauty but never had occasion to tell her of his feelings toward her. However, on one of his visits to her home to deal with some problems related to her Sunday school class, she told Pastor Mainer that she felt a strong attraction to him. It was something she had felt for quite some time, and though she didn't think she had any problems in her marriage, she had reached the point where she felt that she had to tell him.

Pastor Mainer was grateful for the natural opportunity to share with Cherie that he, too, had similar feelings for her. He viewed their attraction as basically a positive and good experience, perfectly acceptable within the context of Christian concern and love. He explained:

> I said to her that since we were both Christians, I really felt that we had something going together whereby we could be open and we could talk through our feelings and channel what I thought were pretty human, natural emotions in some kind of positive way.

He then recommended to Cherie that the best course for them was to meet weekly for counseling during which times they could talk about the meaning of their mutual attraction to one another. He also said to Cherie:

> You know it is good to get these feelings out, because I've kept them secret. I really don't plan to do anything with them. I enjoy being with you, but now that we have both shared this I think what we ought to do is continue right away to talk about these feelings and what they have meant to our family and to ourselves and what this will mean to our relationship in the time to come.

With an obvious show of reluctance, Cherie agreed to the weekly counseling sessions.

Pastor Mainer's purpose in the counseling sessions with Cherie was to arrive at some kind of perspective so he could continue being a pastor to her as well as a friend. They met three times. The first appointment, after the disclosure of their mutual attraction, was in Pastor Mainer's office. Mainer kept the sessions to an hour in length and preferred meeting at his office instead of in her home. However, Cherie felt uncomfortable meeting in his office, so the last two sessions were in her home.

The whole venture ended on a disappointing note for

several important reasons. After the third counseling interview Cherie proposed that they drop the counseling, forget the whole matter, and just say "Hi" when they saw each other in the future. She said she didn't see any benefit in continuing to talk about their feelings. So that ended the counseling, and Pastor Mainer and Cherie now have a politely proper, cold relationship. As Pastor Mainer observed, "Things did not really work out too constructively."

Theologically, Pastor Mainer had seen this experience as an opportune occasion to say something positive to Cherie about sexuality. He had explained to her that he wanted her to feel O.K. about her attraction to him, and to view sexual attraction as a gift of God that is dangerous if it gets out of hand, but beautiful in the way it draws people closer together. He intended to have her accept her sexual feelings by his self-affirmation of his own attraction to her.

But in addition to his theological reasons, Pastor Mainer later was aware that his well-sounding intentions may have been mixed with a simple interest in finding a way to spend more time with Cherie in order to enjoy his attraction to her.

> I really had a difficult time, as I look back on it, filtering through my real feelings. I wasn't sure whether I was as idealistic as I thought in trying to help her and help myself. Maybe I just wanted to use that counseling idea as a way to continue to be with her.

Critique

Pastor Mainer's experience is instructive because it illustrates how well-meaning pastors may easily lead their counselees and themselves in a fruitless direction.

His error was in making their mutual sexual attraction the principal focus of the counseling. By doing this, he had really changed the fundamental structure of his pastoral relationship to Cherie. In effect they had become "lovers" with a beautiful gift trying to figure out how to be friends and pastor-parishioner. By the third session Cherie had become disillusioned with an "affair" having that kind of agenda and decided she wanted it to end.

By contrast, in the context of a professional pastoral relationship, the basic structure never changes regardless of what issues are discussed. Feelings of mutual sexual attraction are treated as are any other feelings that occur in the counseling. They are openly explored for the counselee's personal learning and/or for uncovering obstacles blocking the counseling process. In such a context the pastor's sexual attraction is reported with the attitude, "Yes, I am attracted to you. Now, how can that data help you explore and deal more effectively with your problems?" and not with the attitude, "Gee, what a neat relationship we have now that we have admitted we are attracted to each other."

Despite Pastor Mainer's good intentions, he never escaped the latter position with Cherie. The whole effort was probably irretrievably lost when he capitulated to Cherie in having their last two sessions in her home. Had he insisted upon having the meetings in his office, despite whatever discomfort she had in meeting there, the clear message to her could have been:

> I am not above all else your lover and accidentally your pastor. I am first of all your pastor, and none of our feelings can change that fact. We shall meet in my office so our relationship can be very clear on that point.

But apparently Pastor Mainer's preoccupation with his attraction to Cherie obscured that point for him, so consequently it was never effectively made for her benefit.

OTHER COMMON PROBLEMS

It is natural for a pastor to be embarrassed about his sexual feelings toward a counselee. In fact, a pastor may be so embarrassed that it may be difficult for him to consider alternatives in deciding what will be best for the counselee.

It may be helpful to understand that there is hardly anything more personal for us as human beings than the sexual feelings we have for another person. We are embarrassed because it is indeed the ultimate disclosure to say, "I am sexually attracted to you. I really like you." Even after many years of marriage, some couples are still embarrassed to say those words to each other. We may feel defenseless and vulnerable when we admit that we have strong feelings of attraction, even within the intimacy of a marriage. So it should not be regarded as unusual that there will be times when a pastor will feel embarrassed by the fact that he is attracted to a counselee.

Another possible source of the pastor's embarrassment, however, may be more within his own control. This would be true if the pastor has an image of himself as minister that does not allow for any expression of his sexuality. He permits himself to enjoy sex with his wife, but to have any other sexual response would be tantamount to a transgression of his ordination vows! Then what a shocking embarrassment it is when he discovers in his study that all his masculinity is not bound by the

burden of such ordination vows! Any natural embarrassment over his feelings is then further aggravated by his
professional embarrassment, thus making it more difficult to focus on what is best for the counselee. A revised
and more realistic view of one's self-image as a pastor
and as a man may help a pastor deal directly with this
level of embarrassment.

*Another problem for a pastor is the risk of how a
counselee will respond if he acknowledges his attraction to her.* The chances for misunderstanding will be
much more remote if from the outset of the counseling
the pastor has specified that the relationship will be
structured within certain limits. If a pastor gives the
impression, whether intending to or not, that the counseling relationship will be casual, that there is no professional, pastoral purpose, and that the two of them are
meeting simply as friends, a woman may very easily
misinterpret an expression of the pastor's sexual feelings as a subtle "proposition," an invitation to move the
"friendship" toward increased intimacy. To avoid such
a misunderstanding, it is imperative for the pastor to
say, in essence: "Whatever feelings I may have toward
you will not change our counseling relationship. I have
no intention of doing anything more about my feelings
than discussing them with you."

*A pastor also must often handle a counseling rela-
tionship involving a secretary or other staff person with
whom he works throughout the week.* It is natural that
some feelings of affection may arise between a pastor
and a woman on his church staff or one of his church
boards if they work closely together. Moreover, it is
common for such a person to approach the pastor for
guidance during a time of personal stress. Then there
arises the problem of how to set limits to a relationship

where there is much personal contact in the routine of their work.

In Pastor Carter's situation, his secretary, Mae, requested his help in dealing with a personal family problem. Mae was a member of the congregation and had been the church secretary for several years. Although Mae was the same age as Pastor Carter, he had not felt any particularly strong attraction to her up to the time she asked him for help.

When Mae said she had a problem she wanted to work on, Pastor Carter recommended that she stay after work once a week for a one-hour counseling session. The counseling continued for about three months, and at some points Mae's husband was also asked to come to the sessions. The main accomplishment in the counseling for Mae was that she came to see herself more as an adult apart from the dominance of her mother. Pastor Carter described it this way:

> I think Mae made good progress. Probably the thing that comes to mind is that she began to open up in all her relationships, and to warm up, and to kind of mature now into a woman rather than being mother's daughter.

This process of maturation for Mae was also a turn-on for the pastor. From his viewpoint he was no longer relating to a little girl but to a woman whom he had helped considerably, and who now enjoyed warm, expressive relationships—particularly with him. Mae's attraction to Pastor Carter became quite evident as she shared with him her various fantasies and dreams during the process of the counseling. Thus, when the counseling sessions were terminated, Pastor Carter's problem was how to work with a parishioner toward whom he was genuinely sexually attracted and who also was attracted to him.

In order to cope with this situation the pastor found it necessary to impose certain limits. He acknowledges that he has not resolved his feelings of attraction for Mae. They are still real and present for him. He has told Mae that he is attracted to her. They have even hugged one another on a few occasions. But they have been open about their feelings so they both may have a clearer awareness about what is going on between them.

Mainly, however, Pastor Carter adheres to what he calls the principle of "benign neglect." He does that by not intentionally cultivating the amorous dimension of their relationship. During office hours there is little casual conversation except during a brief coffee break. There are no long, open-ended conversations. Their main purpose at the office is to get the work done, and that purpose defines the nature of the relationship. Moreover, Pastor Carter is careful to see that they do not dwell on their interpersonal relationship by repeated discussion of their attraction for each other. At his suggestion, the social contacts between the two couples have been reduced to a minimum so he and Mae will actually see less of each other. Benign neglect in effect means that Pastor Carter and Mae have been open about saying they are attracted to each other, but that dimension of their relationship is simply acknowledged without further overt encouragement.

A pastor's attraction to a woman on his church staff is best handled by keeping their relationship well-defined by the purpose of their work. Whether or not they discuss the sexual and affectional dimensions of their relationship, their interaction can be structured with sufficient limits if the pastor has determined within himself that their work and not their personal attraction will be the sole basis on which they manage their personal contacts.

Finally, if a pastor never deals openly with a counselee about his attraction to her, there are several considerations he should remember.

1. Insofar as possible, maintain a candid self-awareness of the intensity of the attraction. Pastors invite problems when they try to ignore sexual feelings that in fact they know are very real.

2. The pastor should have a friend, a professional consultant, or a support group with whom he can comfortably talk about these feelings. The pastor who is willing to be open about this matter with a trusted confidante may find some invaluable help for both himself and the counselee, and maybe even avoid some serious problems he may have been blind to.

3. Purposeful self-awareness and consulting with another counselor will aid the pastor in avoiding playing subtle sex games with the counselee. Where an attraction is strongly felt, the natural tendency is to play flirting games designed or intended to arouse the reciprocal interest of the other person. This will not be in the best interest of the counselee or the pastor.

4. If the pastor's sexual feelings are interfering with his counseling, and if he does not see any constructive way to deal with the issue, he should refer her to another counselor. There will be obvious clues, if the pastor wants to acknowledge them, that his attraction to the counselee is inhibiting his effectiveness as a counselor: continuing obvious discomfort and anxiety during the counseling sessions; poor concentration interrupted by sexual fantasies; continuing casual chitchat with the woman without addressing the real issues that brought her to counseling; signs of overpoliteness toward the

woman, avoidance of confrontation and fear of displeasing her; preoccupation with thoughts and fantasies about the counselee between sessions; and obvious anticipation of the next appointment coupled with fears that she may terminate the counseling and not return. The recurrence of these clues should give the pastor good reason to consider seriously referring the woman to another counselor.

If the pastor's attraction to the woman is a source of private enjoyment that does not intrude upon the best interests of the parishioner, or provide an escape from his marriage, or interfere with his professional functioning as a pastor, then by all means he should allow himself that singular pleasure, rejoicing that he too belongs to the natural order of God's beautiful creation!

5
The Pastor
Deals with His Wife

> Indeed, this is the miracle of dialogue: it can bring
> relationship into being, and it can bring into being
> once again a relationship that has died. There is only
> one qualification to these claims for dialogue: it must
> be mutual and proceed from both sides, and the par-
> ties to it must persist relentlessly.—Reuel L. Howe[39]

PASTOR HANKS slowly pulled the church door shut.
Lost in his thoughts, he walked across the dark parking
lot to his car. He was vaguely aware of unlocking the car
door and putting the key in the ignition. His mind was
sorting through a flurry of questions. Mary Parsons had
just left his office. He had been seeing her for counseling
on her marriage for the last five weeks. Although he had
tried to dismiss his initial feelings in the first couple of
weeks, it was all too clear to him now. Mary Parsons was
pretty, even sexy, and tonight she had said four times,
if not eight, how grateful she was for his help. She just
couldn't have survived if she hadn't been able to lean
on him for strength.

Pastor Hanks turned the key in the ignition. "But I
am a married man. I love my wife! What the hell is
going on with me?" He pulled on his headlights and
pointed the car toward the street. "I'm worse than a
teen-ager falling in love for the first time when I'm

around Mary—it's plain stupid. But what am I going to do? I wonder what Alice would say." The car turned into the driveway, the two beams of light revealing a tricycle and a wagon guarding the entrance to the garage. "I wish the kids would put those things away," he grumbled. "I think I could handle this a lot better if I didn't feel like I was keeping something from Alice. After all, I haven't done anything wrong, and furthermore I have no intention of doing anything. I wonder how Alice would take this if she really knew."

An hour and a half later, Pastor Hanks turned off the bedside light. The darkness brought an awesome silence. In spite of his cheery attempts at conversation when he got home, Alice could tell something was bothering him. Then, deciding there was far more to be gained than to be lost, he took a deep breath and began: "Honey, I want to tell you something I've been thinking about for a while. It's about the sessions I've been having with Mary Parsons. Do you feel like talking now?"

Later, he remembered the feeling he had about what he and Alice said to each other that night in bed.

> I can remember the feeling of that conversation. We talked for quite a while. I have more of a memory of the feeling, the good feeling of being able to share this with my wife and talking it through, than I do of any details of exactly what I said. I had nothing to feel guilty about. I hadn't accepted any invitation, implied or otherwise. It had been purely a mind kind of thing that I could be open with my wife about and simply say I had some problems here, but I was working with them and thought I could handle it all right. But I wanted her to know.
>
> I saw it as an opportunity to reinforce an open-

ness between my wife and me that we were working on. I looked at this as an opportunity to say to my wife rather directly, "I want to be open with you, a 'no secrets' kind of thing."

A pastor's attraction to a counselee always involves his wife in some way. Whether or not he ever discusses the matter with her, sexual attraction to another woman often implies some degree of possible marital infidelity. For some parsonage couples feelings of attraction for other persons are not a serious problem so long as the feelings are not acted on. But for other parsonage couples the mere presence of such feelings for someone other than one's spouse is a serious threat that should not even be talked about except in superficial references.

It can be a major turning point in any marriage when both partners discover they can be sexually attracted to persons other than their spouse. This learning about human nature can crush some idealistic views about what it means to be in love and married. To be attracted to someone outside the marriage becomes a special problem for the parsonage, since many pastors do work a great deal with women.

There is always the question of trust. Can the wife trust her husband with the counselees? Can the husband trust his wife to understand the kinds of feelings he is experiencing? How can the pastor's wife be a source of genuine support to her husband when she's feeling insecure about her place as his woman? Should the husband come directly home from every counseling session with a woman and report?

This chapter will not offer explicit answers to all these complex questions. Each pastor and his wife need to work through their own unique approach to these problems together. But in these pages we can examine in depth some of the major dimensions of these problems which may be blocking a pastor and his wife from being of the most help to each other.

Examining the Problems

Many pastors never say anything to their wives when they are attracted to a counselee. In fact, when Pastor Kurtz was asked by his wife if he thought the counselee was attractive, he flatly denied it, but his wife suspected he was hiding something. The counselee was a sixteen-year-old girl in the youth group, and a good friend to both of them. The girl was what Pastor Kurtz described as "sexually potent and attractive. She was the kind of person that has always been attractive to me—dark hair, shapely, flirtatious, with a manner that says, 'Let's get better acquainted.' "

Pastor Kurtz and his wife would talk about the girl's way of attracting the attention of the men in the church, and on some occasions his wife would say that she knew her husband, too, found the girl attractive. Pastor Kurtz recalled, "I remember that I would defensively deny it." His wife's reply then was an accusation that if he never had any thoughts about the girl, then he wouldn't be so emphatic about his denial! They never discussed the matter any farther; the husband maintained his denial and his wife maintained her disbelief in his denial.

When a pastor decides not to say anything to his wife about a counselee he is attracted to, there may be several reasons for not bringing up the subject. Some pastors would never tell their wives about a particular counselee because of a general rule not to discuss any church business with their wives. Many pastors feel it would be breaking the bond of confidentiality with the counselee even to mention to their wives that the woman came for counseling. For these pastors any feelings they have toward a female counselee could never be spoken of at home because it would violate the trust placed in them by the counselee.

Another reason pastors do not talk with their wives about this matter is that they are afraid the wife will become upset and attribute more significance to the husband's feelings than he does. Pastor Baldwin and his wife had been married four years, and the counselee was a young woman about ten years younger than he. After two or three sessions, he was aware of a definite attraction on his part for her. He told his wife the woman was seeing him for counseling, but he did not tell his wife about the sexual response he felt during the counseling sessions. His reasoning for not saying more was, "I suppose I was afraid that my wife would make too much of it, that she would not be able to accept that I had such feelings."

Pastor Morton found himself in a little different situation. The woman he was attracted to was a church leader, and because of her particular responsibilities in the church she and the pastor spent several hours together every week. In other situations where he had felt attraction, Pastor Morton had talked about his feelings with his wife, and she had always been understanding. But in those cases he and the counselee were meeting for a stated single purpose, and Pastor Morton felt his wife could understand that. But with the woman who was a church leader and whom he saw so often he felt his wife would find that harder to understand. He was afraid, he said, that he would put doubt in his wife's

mind, and that she would misinterpret why he was seeing the woman so much on church business.

Likewise, Pastor Morril didn't tell his wife about a
counselee to whom he was attracted because he feared
she would reason like this: If it was important enough
for him to tell her, then it must really be a problem. He
was attracted to the woman, but he didn't want unduly
to stir up his wife's imagination and risk her misinter-
pretation that there was more to his feelings than there
really was.

Some pastors do not tell their wives because they are
sure the wife would be too upset or threatened. Pastor
Clinton feels this way about his wife.

> Sometimes I feel that I'm overprotective of my
> wife in some regards. But she has some feelings
> of insecurity, and I just don't want to give her
> cause to feel any more insecure than she, for
> some reason or other, already feels. So I haven't
> really said, "Hey, this gal really turns me on." She
> gets a little perturbed once in a while, you know,
> if I even look at someone.

Another pastor thought his wife's self-image would be
crushed if she were to find out he occasionally had feelings of attraction to another woman. He wasn't sure,
but he didn't want to run the risk of telling her to find
out if he were wrong.

> I think she would be hurt. I think her self-con-
> cept would really suffer. I think it would crush
> her. I don't know. Maybe she sees it as perfectly
> normal. I'm not about to find out.

Sometimes a pastor may simply feel that his wife
really does not care enough about him or about his
feelings to listen to him. It is not unusual for a pastor to
sense his wife's indifference if their marriage has been

marked by tension and arguing. In one such instance a pastor felt his secretary was far more open to his various feelings than his wife would be. Still another wife has told her husband that she gets too upset hearing about things like sexual feelings for other people. She has plainly said she does not want to deal with those matters.

> I'm sure it would be very upsetting to my wife. She does know and has been upset at times when I've suggested that I have sexual feelings toward other people. It's something she doesn't like to hear, doesn't want to deal with.
>
> This situation with this counselee represents a part of me that my wife will perhaps never know in any specific way. To tell her would be more troubling than it is worth, frankly.

Some pastors also don't tell their wives because they are scared! Pastor Thompson and his wife have exchanged a few kidding remarks about an attractive counselee he is seeing, but he didn't say any more about his real feelings because he didn't want to stir up her jealousy. "Maybe I was just scared she would pounce on me!" Pastor Dorner was sure he didn't tell his wife about his attraction to a counselee because he was afraid. As he put it, he was certain she would have become an "outraged mate."

Sometimes a pastor's personal sense of shame may inhibit him from acknowledging to his wife that he has felt some attraction to a counselee. Early in Pastor Lichert's ministry a woman just a few years older than he came for help with an alcohol problem. During the first several counseling sessions it developed that the woman had a history of promiscuous relationships with several men. Near the end of the third session she said that her sexual drive was such a problem for her that she even wanted to have sex with Pastor Lichert. At that moment Pastor Lichert became quite anxious because he was suddenly aware of thinking it would be a good idea. Because he was so threatened by the situation, and because he ordinarily refers alcohol problems, he promptly referred this woman to a psychologist. He mainly remembers that at that early stage in his ministry he felt very uncomfortable about being so attracted to a counselee. He really felt ashamed about his feelings, and that was his explanation for why he did not relate the incident to his wife. As he put it, "I suppose that the main reason I did not tell my wife was that I was ashamed at having those sexual feelings toward another woman."

In some cases the very nature of the minister's marriage does not allow for the discussion of the pastor's feelings toward counselees. One pastor was sure it would threaten the marriage if he were to be honest about the sexual fantasies he has had about different women in the church. He says flatly, "I don't think it would be beneficial to our relationship for me to start talking about my fantasizing with other women." In another instance a pastor said he couldn't talk about such things to his wife. He attributed it to a deficiency in the marriage: "It points to a lack of intimacy in the marriage. We don't have that kind of intimacy." So they don't discuss the matter openly, and he just assumes that she knows he has such experiences and trusts him to handle them discreetly. But he does not know that for sure.

Many pastors don't tell their wives about every instance when they are attracted to a counselee because it is something about which they have talked at other times and have reached some mutual understanding. For Pastor Carney his counseling for over two years with a vivacious, talented, and physically attractive woman did not require any special comment to his wife because they both know there will be times when each of them will find others attractive.

> My wife has been aware, particularly in terms of working out our own professional roles as well as our relationship with each other, that she's in situations of contact with males her own age and I'm in contact continually with females my own age. She knows that physical attraction and more than physical attraction in terms of the real kind of feelings that you have for one another is a fact of life we both have to deal with.
>
> Because my wife knows the counselee and knows the counselee is attractive, she would know that I would be attracted to that person, but we didn't need to talk about it.

Indirect communication between a pastor and his wife may indicate both know how the pastor feels about a counselee. Sometimes a pastor may feel that, without having to say anything, his wife knows that he is attracted to a woman seeing him for counseling. Pastors speak of a nonverbal or intuitive communication between themselves and their wives, so they are quite certain their wives know how they feel. Another kind of indirect communication occurs when a pastor may say in an offhand manner that the woman is attracted to him, or has hugged him, but he doesn't say that he is also attracted to her. Husbands may also send an indirect message by becoming more sexually attentive to their wives, either out of guilt or because their sexual interests have been stimulated during a recent session with the counselee.

There is always some risk when a pastor is honest with his wife about his sexual feelings toward other women. Thoroughgoing honesty in a marriage or any intimate relationship carries with it the clear risk that there may be misunderstandings and hurt feelings. But there always exists the possibility for good to come when the risk is taken. Pastors have found both positive and disappointing consequences growing out of talking with their wives about counselees to whom they are attracted.

This chapter began with the experience of Pastor Hanks. He decided to tell Alice about his feelings toward Mary Parsons. But it was a risk, because their marriage had been through some hard times and they were just beginning to get things on a sure footing again. Early in their marriage their relationship had been pretty superficial. Then there were tragic experiences, including periods of hospitalization, that put even more strain on the marriage. But instead of being divisive, the situation symbolized for them one more opportunity for sharing and supporting each other. It meant for them that their marriage was becoming more stable. Alice told him that night that she was glad he had told her. It meant a deepening of their mutual relationship that he would be that honest and trusting. She expressed genuine concern about how he planned to handle his feelings in the future with Mary, particularly if she made a direct pass at him. Nonetheless, Alice was glad they had been able to talk about it.

In Pastor Farr's situation the risk was how his wife would react. As it turned out she found it hard to deal with, but there were some good things that happened too. Beverly was about eight years older than Pastor Farr, and she came to him for counseling related to a serious accident in which she had been involved. This was certainly not the first time Pastor Farr had found a parishioner attractive, but Beverly was an extraordinarily pretty woman. When she came to one of the counseling sessions she was wearing a low-cut dress with a peekaboo kind of blouse. Her breasts were particularly evident, and Pastor Farr found it quite difficult to concentrate on what she was saying.

It was a quite threatening experience for him. He had never felt such a strong attraction to a counselee before even though he had been in the ministry for nearly ten years. In fact, because the incident bothered him so much, he decided it would be worth the risk to share it with his wife. He didn't want something like this to jeopardize their marriage in any possible way.

It was difficult for both of them to talk about it. His wife was clearly upset to learn that her husband could have such intense sexual feelings toward another woman. Also, knowing he had those kinds of feelings made her wonder what he would do in the future with some of his counselees. Yet, in spite of her doubt and concern she let her husband know she accepted what had happened, and she was glad, basically, that they could talk about it. Pastor Farr realized his wife felt uncomfortable about the matter, but he also felt good that they had been honest with each other. His wife's acceptance gave him a deep sense of support.

> There's some gospel in that for me, that the human being and woman I'm closest to can accept me as a man with attractions for other women besides her. I feel guilty about that when I feel that kind of attraction strongly.

And he went on to say he felt their marriage was stronger because they could be honest with each other about his feelings for the counselee. "It's just a degree of openness and of better understanding that we have with each other now."

For still another minister, Pastor Kane, there were some reservations in his mind afterward that perhaps he had told his wife too much. The Kanes are in the middle stage of life, their children are grown and away from the home, and they are really rediscovering each other and making a new marriage for themselves. Formerly he had been married essentially to the church, and his wife had reared the family. Now they are both trying their best to make a new, vital relationship between themselves after twenty years or so of avoiding each other.

The counselee, about twenty years younger than Pastor Kane, is one of the most beautiful women he has ever known: "She has a beautiful figure, lovely breasts, is exquisitely feminine, her eyes just seem to twinkle." And besides being so attractive, she seems to have everything in her personality that he has missed in his wife. "My wife will never be the sensitive, gentle type of person that I would like. As I get older I need more of the gentleness that is reflected in the counselee."

Pastor Kane said that it was easier for him to tell his wife about the counselee because, as they have been working on their new marital relationship, they have been talking more about what sex means for each of them at their age. So, early in the counseling relationship with the woman, he came home one afternoon and said, "Who do you suppose came in today?" Then he went on to add: "She really did things to me." "What things?" his wife inquired. He went into some more detail about how hard it had been for him to keep his mind on what the counselee had been talking about. His wife replied, "Why, you dirty old man! At your age!"

She wanted to know, "Do you have those same feelings with me?" Then he elaborated at some length on the ways he found the counselee attractive, and also pointed up how he wished his wife might respond in some new ways in their relationship.

The impact of their honest sharing with each other was a realization for both of them that their sexuality was just as vital to them now as it had been years before. They both agreed to exercise and slim down for each other, and he has also noted more sexual interest toward him on the part of his wife. She is even taking some initiatives toward him, which she had never done before in their marriage!

However, Pastor Kane has mixed feelings about how much he shared with his wife. He feels his wife is basically insecure, and he's afraid that more information about his feelings toward the counselee would be too threatening and unsettling. His wife once commented that she had heard of husbands leaving their wives for other women, and consequently, she thought he could easily do that too. "So I had planted insecurity here, I think. If I had just not been quite as free in how much I told her, it probably would have been healthier for her."

RECOMMENDATIONS FOR PARSONAGE COUPLES

Assess your marriage. When one pastor went through a difficult two-month period sorting out his feelings for a parishioner who was also a close friend, he attributed his ability to cope to the positive way he and his wife were relating to each other.

> When I did have these sexual feelings about the counselee, even a couple of times when I was in

bed with my wife and I was thinking about the counselee, I remember vividly that the love my wife and I had for each other tended to help me overcome those thoughts. Had my wife and I been having a real struggle sexually or emotionally at that time, I'm quite sure my reaction to those sexual thoughts and feelings would have been much different. My ability to react positively in that situation was greatly affected by my relationship at home.

Neither a husband nor a wife can assess their own marriage if they are looking for someone to blame. First of all, a partner who feels blamed naturally becomes defensive and starts finding fault with the mate. Then there is small chance for positive mutual conversation between them. Secondly, when one is putting blame on the other, there is little openness to recognize one's own personal contribution to the marriage and its problems. Instead of blaming, it is better to acknowledge that both have had a major part in making the marriage what it is. It takes considerable maturity to look at one's marriage in that way, but it is the only way to find out what is really happening between a minister and his wife. So regardless of the nature of marital tension, both partners need to discover their own part in making the marriage what it is.

It is probably also true that if a counselee becomes a serious threat to a parsonage marriage, there were underlying problems with the marriage before the counselee came along. A pastor or his wife might prefer to deceive themselves with the excuse that if a third party had not intruded, the marriage would have been just fine. Generally, if a pastor's relationship with a counselee becomes disruptive to him and his wife, they need to examine the other dimensions of their marriage. One pastor had the insight to recognize that his attraction to a parishioner was simply a red light, as he put it. He was not investing himself enough in his marriage at home. He knows he is copping out, and in fact when he works at his marriage things do get better. Another pastor said, "I know that through the years I have run from domestic conflicts at home to get more involved in church and community responsibilities." Becoming preoccupied with a counselee can simply be a convenient way to avoid the problems a minister has with his wife.

A parsonage marriage, particularly, should have the capacity to be flexible and adaptive to changes in each partner. A marriage is always changing because both persons are changing and their particular needs and interests are continually changing. Because of that, if a couple tries to maintain the same "contract" under which they originally married, they will certainly encounter difficulties as each of them continues to develop as a person.

Charlotte Clinebell has told about a couple that came for counseling because the wife was unhappy. Her husband was saying, "Why can't she be happy? She has everything she wants." He was genuinely bewildered by his wife's discontent. She was too. Both had decided that it was her problem. It turned out that she was simply bored. The woman had begun to develop new interests, activities that took her more outside the home. She was making a life for herself, but these new developments on her part clashed sharply with her husband's firm notions of what a woman "should" be. Reluctantly, they were finally divorced. Clinebell correctly emphasizes: "No one contract is good for the lifetime of a marriage unless it can change as needs, interests, and desires change."[40]

A minister who had an affectionate relationship with a parishioner for several years attributed his extramarital interest in part to the fact that his original marriage contract didn't fit his new, developing needs as a person.

> When I was married, I think that my contract was that I needed a woman who would be faithful, a virgin, righteous, a good housekeeper. Someone I could trust. And at that point I wasn't sure who I was. When I married I was a very unsure person with little confidence. I needed positive strokes in order to keep going. I hated to be criticized.
>
> So I married my wife, and she gave me all those security blankets. After I was married for ten years I discovered the original contract was lapsing and my needs were different. My need ten years later was for much more affection, sexuality, much more openness in our relationship, and affirmation that my wife either wasn't able or willing to give. So I sought that fulfillment with the parishioner.

Both the pastor and his wife will develop many new interests and needs through the years of marriage. The healthy marriage is not shocked by such changing needs and finds ways—sometimes with genuine pain and sacrifice for both—but finds ways to accommodate those changing needs within the framework of the marriage.

"If my wife were more sexy, I wouldn't have any problems with counselees. I bring home books on sex, but she won't read them." These are not uncommon complaints from pastors, and behind them one can well imagine a parsonage wife considering herself frigid, feeling guilty, and not understanding why she doesn't feel sexy when he comes home after doing the Lord's work for fifteen hours. Older husbands have learned that the way to sexual happiness is not paved with the latest book they bring home for their wives. A wife properly resents this hardly subtle suggestion that if she reads the right book she'll get straightened out sexually. By now we know that it is quite normal for a husband and wife to go through times of sexual tension when one partner is not sufficiently accommodating to the other's needs—that happens both ways. It is not always just parsonage husbands who don't get enough sex! Enduring or recurring sexual problems should be a signal that the couple needs to work on the relationship. They should not be an excuse for using counselees to satisfy one's sexual needs. The pastor who finds fault with his wife's coolness may do well to examine himself as a marriage partner and patient, wooing lover.

Is it possible for each partner to say to the other: "Our marriage relationship means more to me than any other relationship I have, and despite the problem areas in our marriage, I want to work with you at improving our marriage"? For some pastors and their wives that frankly may be very difficult for them to say. The pain and anger they feel may have been building up for too many years. Now they may not really care to work any longer on the marriage. That tragic description fits many a parsonage marriage that, by sheer granite determination, is made to appear calm on the surface to an unsuspecting congregation.

If a marriage is to continue meeting each person's needs, both spouses need to know that the other is committed 100 percent to making the marriage better. There is no substitute for saying: "Our marriage is precious to me even though I was hopping mad at you this morning for being so insensitive to me last night! But I would like to try to get to the bottom of this issue if you care to talk about it now." Actions, too, can say in a thousand different ways that the marital relationship really matters. The husband who calls home to say he'll be twenty minutes late is saying, "I'm thinking of you even though I've had a hectic day today." When a parishioner calls three minutes before supper, the husband who says, "I'll call you back in an hour" instead of talking for twenty minutes then sends a clear message about his priorities—to both the parishioner and his wife. The pastor who clears his weekly schedule to have a date with his wife for dinner without the children, or just spending a quiet evening at home together has surely said without words what volumes could never describe! And though a husband may be embarrassed to show affection in public, holding her hand or putting an arm around her waist at the congregational dinner can be quite affirming to a parsonage wife!

How can a wife say to her husband that their relationship matters to her above all else? Well, by saying it out loud, for starters. Surprising as it may seem, she may say the relationship really matters by occasionally blowing her stack. Pretense about feelings may only perpetuate the illusion of tranquillity. Also, a wife who is willing to listen to her husband unload about his day without giving advice may be saying very effectively that their relationship is very important to her.

Honest assessment of a parsonage marriage is the first necessary step for dealing with a pastor's attraction to a counselee. The chief focus then stays where it belongs:

not on a problem parishioner but on how to enrich the parsonage marriage. Within the context of a marriage in which both husband and wife value each other and their relationship, there can be constructive steps for dealing with the husband's sexual feelings toward a counselee.

Husband and wife will recognize and accept the difficulty each may have in talking about sexual feelings. If a couple has never discussed the possibility that either one of them could be attracted to another person, the first several times they talk about it may be awkward. Getting into the subject may first be accompanied with joking or some casual remarks about sex. One minister and his wife found it helpful to take turns listing, 1 through 5, the persons most attractive to them in the congregation. This technique made it less embarrassing for each of them to admit they found others sexually attractive.

A couple will find it easier to speak of their extramarital attractions when they realize that such attractions are common, normal, and not a breach of their marriage vows. When a husband and wife can accept this about each other, they may experience much relief from their guilt about having such feelings.

As a parsonage couple begin to talk about their sexuality, and particularly about sexual feelings they have toward other persons, it is important that they both say to what extent they want to talk about the matter. It is the kind of subject that both husband and wife must be equally willing to explore. One partner may find it too threatening or distressing to talk about very often. Those feelings should be respected. Certainly failure ever to talk about this area may maintain tensions that should be resolved. Both partners need to be willing to look at a difficult issue if it is to be dealt with productively.

When a mate listens to a spouse relate deep feelings about sex, it is helpful not to ask too many questions to try to "analyze" the reasons for the feelings. When sensitive feelings are briskly explained away or treated indifferently with a stream of questions, a person can feel put down. Each person needs to be heard and appreciated, and this may require much patience and tolerance from both partners. If a husband says that he has often had sexual fantasies and dreams and his wife says she rarely has, it is insensitive for him to insist that she must have had them. If that has been her experience, then it has been her experience. Contradicting her may end the conversation and make future talk about her feelings unlikely.

Insofar as possible, a couple should allow each other to share any negative feelings each has about the other's extramarital attractions. A husband or a wife may actually feel jealous, angry, or hurt because the other is sexually attracted outside the marriage. Generally it is better for the marriage if partners can be open about their negative reactions.

"But won't I drive him away if he knows how bothered I am?" Open channels of communication require the risks of being forthright. "Yes, I feel insecure when you tell me your counselee turns you on, but I would rather have us be able to talk about it, difficult as it is sometimes, than be shut off from each other." A husband may be reluctant to talk with his wife if he feels he needs to protect her from becoming upset. One pastor put it this way:

> I wish the relationship between my wife and me
> were such that I could confidently discuss some-

thing like this with her without feeling it would upset her and give her more muscle spasms in her back than she already has.

A wife needs to consider whether she needs that kind of "protection." Also, some husbands might be quite surprised to find out their wives are more willing than they suspected to have them talk about their sexual feelings toward counselees. It may be just a handy excuse for a husband to cut off communication with the rationalization that his wife will fall apart if she knows the truth about his sexuality.

Once a parsonage couple begins to level on this whole subject, surprising things may turn up. A pastor may hear about his wife's feeling abandoned and forgotten when he has been all too willing to respond to the call of some other woman. A husband may discover his wife has been more sensitive to this issue than he had wanted to acknowledge!

Learning to deal with the future. Unless a minister leaves the pastorate, and unless he stops counseling women, there will probably be future occasions when he will have definite sexual thoughts and feelings about a counselee. Neither husband nor wife will be helped if either one feels that every incident must be reported and discussed. The childish dimensions of such expectations are obvious and will only serve to block effective marital communication.

There are two specific things a pastor can do to reassure his wife and ease communication with her about such future instances. He can make it known to her, if it is in fact the case, that his counseling practice always includes the setting of limits. A wife can feel much more comfortable if she knows that his sessions occur within stated times. A wife will sense with confidence that her husband is in charge of the counseling sessions instead of possibly being controlled or manipulated by developments that may occur during a counseling session. A husband can also reassure his wife by the way he handles phone calls. Excessively long conversations occurring at unsociable hours may easily give a wife the impression that he is not in charge of the situation, and the wife probably is right in her judgment!

The second thing a husband can do to reassure his wife is to make it clear that except for definite emergencies his counselees come second to her and his family. Pastors who have an insatiable need to feel important by playing the dependable rescuer will indeed communicate to their wives that home and family are not very important. Every pastor will have some instances when a counselee needs his attention on the Fourth of July or at 2:30 A.M. But those should be few and far between, particularly with the same counselee. There are not many counseling emergencies that cannot wait till nine the next morning. If a pastor is in fact more attentive to the emergencies of the women in his church than he is to the needs of his wife, he cannot be surprised if she wonders whether his interests are really at home. The sensitive husband best demonstrates that he is in charge of his counseling by effectively demonstrating that his first priority is his wife and family.

Also, it should be made clear to the pastor's wife that she should express her displeasure if she feels she's being replaced by a counselee. If a wife feels closed off in this area of deep feelings, she may well feel closed off in other important areas. If a wife does not want her husband to do any counseling at all with any women, that is an unrealistic expectation for a parish pastor. But if a wife feels her husband is continually preoccupied with another woman in the congregation, she doesn't help him or herself by keeping her observation bottled up. Her strong feelings will probably begin having a negative impact on both herself and the marriage. If, indeed, she has jumped to conclusions or if her feelings of jealousy prove to be unfounded, it is much better that such feelings be discussed openly than left to become an obstacle to other areas of the relationship.

Most importantly, prepare for the future by contracting with each other to plan for growth in the marriage. Many pastors are now leading growth groups for couples in their churches. But being a participant is different from being a leader. A minister and his wife can achieve deeper levels of intimacy with each other if they are in a group of peers instead of parishioners. A short-term marriage growth group meeting once a week for ten to twelve weeks can be invaluable for enriching a parsonage marriage. Likewise, an intensive three- or four-day marriage retreat or workshop can have similar growth benefits.

A parsonage couple can also demonstrate to each other that their relationship is important by planning significant times to be alone together. A vacation for a week or two without the children is an excellent way to rediscover each other. Arrangements for child care during such a period may not be easy, but the trouble is worth the dividends when a man and wife make that kind of serious investment in their marriage.

A good parsonage marriage will never prevent sexual attraction to counselees. But the growing marriage between the pastor and his wife will thrive on the rediscovery of each other as changing, evolving persons. In that context each partner's developing sexual needs and interests will not become a stumbling block but, instead, can be one of many exciting doorways to the deeper enrichment of a vital relationship.

6
A Wife's Response
by Virginia Y. Rassieur

AT THE PARTY, eyes are raised and interest quickens as Chuck answers questions concerning this book about sexual attraction. After the first queries have passed, the wife nearest me pauses in thought and ventures, "And how do *you* feel about his counseling attractive women?" As I take a breath to begin my response, she goes on, herself: "I'm just uncomfortable thinking about my own husband [who is a minister] having to spend much time with other women. I really don't like it." Or she says, "I feel angry about it at times, particularly when their phone calls interrupt us at home." She changes the subject.

My answer to that question cannot be given in a neat sentence or two at a party. Quite obviously the question arouses many feelings within the asker. I have the same feelings and I continue to deal with them. One thing the other wife and I know for sure is that we each ponder quietly the imagined closeness of the counseling relationship and try to picture how our particular husband conducts himself. The rest of the partygoers continue to discuss the high-sounding theological implications of this or that approach. As for me, I'd rather skip the theology and find out just what does go on behind those closed doors.

All sorts of uneasy feelings raise their sassy heads to taunt me when I think of how attractive other women may be to my husband. Suddenly my makeup is all wrong, my hair tousles, my wardrobe is drab, my stomach protrudes unbecomingly, and it's too late to shower before he comes home. My routine has been dull, and I have nothing outstanding to share with him at the end of the day. So I decide just to listen to him because, after all, his job and life are the more important. About then some disc jockey blares out, appropriately he thinks, with the song that goes: "Hey, little girl, with your hair up in curlers . . . Don't you know there are girls at the office? . . . And men will always be men."—Then I growl at the radio and slouch all the more.

That song and those feelings wrong me. They try to convey that the total burden of the success of our marriage (I was tempted to say "my marriage") rests solely upon my shoulders; that somehow if I am always the epitome of a "good" wife ever striving to become a "better" wife, Chuck's head will not be turned at the sight of a youthful, well-put-together female. The fact is that my husband must share equal responsibility for our marriage. And he has to deal with how he acts upon the perfectly natural feelings that come along with his daily contacts with women. I know he finds pleasure in seeing an attractive woman, but he alone determines in an active way what he will do next.

Feeling relieved, I turn off the radio as well as the idea that the marriage is mainly my responsibility, only to turn around aghast at some other ugly realizations. I have absolutely no control over certain aspects of my husband's counseling work. A woman can choose to present herself in whatever alluring garb she likes when she seeks counseling for loneliness. She might even make some kind of pass at him—or, perish the thought, he toward her—and I can do nothing or perhaps will know nothing about it. A less flamboyant woman may need to deal with her sexual life in a counseling session. I can count on that to make a perceptible impression on the maleness of my husband. That is to be expected; it is useless to deny that it happens. I also know my husband well enough to see how he is personally affirmed by feeling strong and being supportive when a woman deals with her dependency needs. All of these, which happen without my permission, seem at first glance to threaten my position in our marital relationship.

I counter these sometimes unmanageable thoughts by dwelling on the elements over which I do exercise some control. For a beginning, my husband and I have sought to communicate fairly openly. Our relationship sours when we do not make the time to share thoughts, experiences, and feelings. From time to time Chuck shares with me his feelings of sexual arousal that occurred during counseling sessions. I picture some wives not wishing to hear about such things. I can understand that, for truly, on my part at least, it does bring about a response deep in my gut to hear them. It was threatening and painful to discuss them at first, but it was preferable to an unspoken agreement to be silent about these feelings. Avoidance magnifies the suspicions and imaginations. It is worth the risk, as a wife, to hear what my husband chooses to share.

The risk is reduced when I consider it in the opposite light. More often than not, I imagine myself in a similar situation, where the roles are reversed and I am the one with the aroused feelings. Then I recognize that these sexual feelings are so normal and natural—a kind of sign that my body is alive to the world around—that merely having them is no great threat.

So my answer is an emphatic yes to the question of whether or not a minister should discuss instances of sexual attraction with his wife. I deeply appreciate the fact that Chuck is aware of himself and his sexual feelings, whether they relate to hiring a new secretary or to dealing with a long-term counseling relationship. We work through the feelings together when either one of us wants to talk about them. I listen to his feelings and he listens to mine. I would resent it if he felt he had to bear these aspects of his counseling alone, lest he make me feel inferior and insecure. If, indeed, my feeling is insecurity, then it is mine to grapple with. Chuck cannot "give" me the feeling of insecurity any more than he can take it away. The unhappy feelings usually occur when we have filled our schedules so full of activity that we have left little time for sharing and intimacies.

I can also exercise the choice to ask my husband about his feelings of attraction to other women. It is unrealistic to imagine that he will have nothing to relate and it eases the way for him to share with me. Despite the threat this suggests, his sharing or my asking him to has eased tensions and turned out to be relieving to both of us.

Becoming aware of and accepting the fact of my own natural sexual response to some men in certain relationships aids me in understanding this same natural response of my husband to other women. No matter how great our relationship happens to be at the time and no matter how completely we have communicated, these are no assurance that other persons will not attract either of us.

At first it took a bit of searching and concentration to

be consciously aware of myself at levels that I usually did not pay attention to on a day-to-day basis. I recall being in a room crowded with chairs where there wasn't much space to move around. As we jostled to take our seats before the meeting began, I spotted our good-looking friend and we made our way over to join him and his wife. My arm and his brushed slightly as we settled and that touch pulled my thoughts into an orbit all their own. As Chuck chatted with the couple, I joyously admitted to myself for the first time in my life that the accidental contact with this other man was both enjoyable and harmless. It was a notable day because I finally acknowledged this in myself. Later I related that new experience to Chuck. I was really affirming myself in revealing to him the awakening I felt.

Of course, that has not been a once-in-a-lifetime experience. The awareness of my own sexual response to men is a continuous unfolding. There have been numerous instances since then in varying degrees—a few of them quite intense—and I expect they will occur again. Some women surely know this about themselves already. Others may have more difficulty in acknowledging a sexual response to men other than their spouses, but I believe it is there within each woman. To become aware at this level we must put aside the early teachings of our culture: that "nice" girls are not sexy; that they do not try to affirm their sexual selves. Getting right down to it, this denial and avoidance of my own sexual response has led me to a confusion of feelings in the past. My buried feelings struggling to make themselves known startled me and clouded my effort to make responsible decisions about my behavior. I found that probing for awareness undercuts the need to flirt and introduces the opportunity to contemplate how to act appropriately.

Now let us deal with the major part of this question over which I readily acknowledge I have no control: my husband. There is no assurance that he will behave and think as I wish he would. In fact, I can be guaranteed otherwise, since he is a quite separate individual from me. My greatest confidence in his making responsible decisions when dealing with other women comes from our marital dialogue, which I have described.

I have no reason, for example, to resent his time spent with attractive women in counseling because I know that they receive his attention only for an hour. Even if they interrupt our family life at home by phoning, I know that the conversation will not survive longer than five or ten minutes. If I feel I am not getting to spend the amount of time I want to with my husband, then I must examine how much time I have allowed in my life for him rather than blame him for spending so much time with "her." I can also request that he make more time for me without getting at all involved in the issue of individual counselees.

Jealousy does not often raise its head because I know that my husband makes a thoughtful effort to limit touching in counseling sessions, and he does not initiate either telephone calls or counseling contacts. I do not pretend that he never touches a counselee in any way —that is unrealistic; but I do trust his effort in keeping both his counseling relationship professional and our marriage primary in importance. I would have difficulty at the gut level if he were to call up an attractive woman counselee other than to cancel an appointment because of illness. Similarly, I would seriously question his motives (personal ones, not theological ones) if he were to suggest that an attractive woman should come to him for counseling rather than let her initiate the counseling need.

I would also like to add a word about sexual fantasies before I conclude. Masters and Johnson wrote an article concerning women and their fantasies in *Redbook Magazine*.[41] Perhaps there is some comfort in knowing that they report that over a period of seventeen years nearly all the women they have worked with have had at least one episode of sexual fantasy in their lifetime. While fantasizing is most active in the younger years, many adults carry over into later years heavy guilt feelings about fantasies. Perhaps this is because many fantasies are conjured up from the very material that constitutes our learned set of inhibitions.

I felt good when the group of women with whom I was meeting dealt with fantasies. We all discovered how normal and natural it is to have them regardless of the wide range our collective fantasies encompassed. Some of the material in my own fantasies comes from instances of awareness of my attraction to men other than my partner. Knowing this about myself, I am comfortable with the expectation that Chuck likely has similar fantasies. His do not threaten our mutual bond any more than mine do.

My main wish for couples working either separately or together on the issue of sexual attraction is that they strive for new sensitivity and understanding with each other. To wives I say that being willing to listen to your husband, even asking him to share his feelings, is only a start. Uncomfortable as it may feel, it is best to hear him level with you because the imagination tends to create worse situations than reality does. Try not to be judgmental, knowing that your own honest sexual response may be similar. Further, risk sharing your reaction to what your husband has to say rather than trying to absorb all he shares. You may get all bottled up.

To husbands, I would hope that your wife is not so fragile as perhaps your view of her may be. Urge lovingly upon her the importance to you for your marriage that you can be open with her in every way. Be willing to hear her express her fears, accept them so she knows she can say them again when they are present. If she is willing to hear you out, then she needs the same kind of ear.

I feel that a wife can and should raise any issues about her husband's counseling that cause her discomfort. If she and her husband openly work on these issues, then it is hoped he can arrange his counseling to show as much consideration for his wife's feelings as he professes to have for the women he counsels.

EPILOGUE
I still
choose you again . . .

I'M GLAD, Ginni, that not many years ago we agreed that our marriage would be based on our continuing to rechoose each other. In effect we decided our marriage would not be a life sentence, but a commitment intentionally reaffirmed each day. Most importantly, that means that I am living with you because I really want to. We also know that that decision is faced by both of us in the numerous relationships we have with others outside our marriage. When you are with other men and I am with other women, we must deal with a continuing choice whether we still want to live with each other. You are still an essential part of my life, and that's why today I choose you again as the one with whom I want to share my life.

I suppose to be honest I have to say that some of the feelings I have occasionally had toward a few counselees did cause me to wonder if I wanted to continue renewing our contract. But I must add that till now no other woman has really made me look at that too seriously. Nonetheless, there have been times of searching in my heart—as probably you too have reflected deeply about your own continuing choice of me.

Today I choose you again for my wife for some reasons that are particularly important to me—reasons that have a lifelong quality. It is important to me that you are an open and growing person. You surely aren't the same person I married! Sometimes I like that and sometimes I don't. We've talked about that, haven't we! But more often than not I like the way you have a firmer grasp on who you are and what you want.

That means you are clearly distinct from me. There isn't that old dependence on me that I think got burdensome for both of us despite how we both thought we liked it. But best of all I like your strength. You aren't made of eggshells. You are able to take care of your own feelings, and knowing that, I feel more comfortable about sharing with you the parts of me I'm more sensitive about.

I choose you again today because you are honest with me. You're honest about your feeling angry and hurt. And when I've lost my perspective on a counselee so you were affected, your honest feedback was what I needed.

I choose you again because you're sexy. You really like your sexuality, more so, I think you would agree, in the last several years. I experience you as being open now not only to your sexual side but also to what it means for me as a man—and especially as your husband —to be sexual. Sure, some other women look pretty interesting to me sometimes, but I honestly doubt they could be any more fun.

And I still choose you because you trust me. No doubt I have to cultivate some of that trust in responsible ways. But you affirm my own innate sense of freedom by your trust, and it is vital for me to claim my own freedom even when I am relating to other women. I choose you because I can trust you too, as you express and live out your freedom. Trust and freedom; they have to go together for us, don't they?

Finally, I choose you because I can't think of anyone else with whom I would rather face the future. The future is so uncertain sometimes. Our feelings are often unpredictable. It's scary to me when I realize we are both changing. What if you stopped choosing me but I still wanted you? I hate to think about that possibility. That's why a part of me wants to control you absolutely so you will always stay just as you are right now. Never change. But how dull! I think that would soon be utterly boring. So go ahead, change. I really want that risk for you and I want it for me.

I choose you again today for the coming years because in our individual freedom I feel we have fashioned a profound commitment to each other, and that gives me a confident feeling about you and about me. It's a confidence that somehow we will deal with the threats that most surely will come to our marriage. It's a confidence that helps me know that I will be able to deal with myself in the close and sometimes intense relationships I will have with others I am trying to help.

I choose you again now because you are really you, and I am I, and the commitment bound up in our individual freedom has become so essential to my being that I had to choose you today, just as now I expect to make the same choice again tomorrow.

NOTES

1. Eric Berne, *Sex in Human Loving* (Simon & Schuster, Inc., 1970), p. 125.

2. Nathaniel S. Lehrman, "The Normality of Sexual Feelings in Pastoral Counseling," *Pastoral Psychology*, Vol. II, No. 105 (June 1960), p. 49.

3. A. A. Brill (ed.), *The Basic Writings of Sigmund Freud* (Random House, Inc., 1938), p. 614.

4. David R. Mace, "Delinquent Sex and Marriage Counselors," *Sexual Behavior*, Vol. I, No. 3 (June 1971), p. 41.

5. Desmond Morris, *Intimate Behaviour* (Random House, Inc., 1971), pp. 9–102.

6. Morton Hunt, *The Affair* (The New American Library of World Literature, Inc., 1971), p. 81.

7. Viktor E. Frankl, *Man's Search for Meaning: An Introduction to Logotherapy* (Pocket Books, Inc., 1963), pp. 206–207.

8. Howard J. Clinebell, Jr., *Basic Types of Pastoral Counseling* (Abingdon Press, 1966), pp. 45–46.

9. Occasions of experience are discrete, indivisible units analyzed by Whitehead as the ultimate particles of nature and human experience. See Cobb's explanation: John B. Cobb, Jr., *A Christian Natural Theology* (The Westminster Press, 1965), pp. 28–39.

10. *Ibid.*, p. 39.

11. *Ibid.*, p. 95.

12. John B. Cobb, Jr., *The Structure of Christian Exis-*

tence (The Westminster Press, 1967), p. 121.

Cobb's analysis is not made without a full consideration of the unconscious dimensions of personality,
which are especially important for any consideration of
human sexual behavior. In fact, it is the elements of the
psyche that the personal "I" of prophetic Judaism does
not control which Cobb asserts the spiritual "I" of Chris-
tianity does assume responsibility for.

"That means that the new spiritual 'I' is responsible
both for what it is and for what it is not, both for what
lies in its power and for what lies beyond its power."
(Cobb, *The Structure of Christian Existence,* p. 124.)

Obviously, Christian existence in the context of such
radical responsibility is inconceivable without the
primacy of God's grace. Cobb calls release from self-
condemnation release from self-preoccupation which is
possible because we are first loved: "Love is, therefore,
on the one hand, the only salvation of the spiritual man
and, on the other hand, unattainable by his own efforts.
The spiritual man can only love when he is freed from
the necessity to love, that is, when he knows himself
already loved in his self-preoccupation. Only if man
finds that he is already accepted in his sin and sickness,
can he accept his own self-preoccupation as it is."
(Cobb, *The Structure of Christian Existence,* p. 135.)

13. Martin Buber, *I and Thou* (Charles Scribner's
Sons, 1970), p. 112.

14. Martin Buber, *I and Thou* (Edinburgh: T. & T.
Clark, 1937), p. 10.

15. Martin Buber, *Between Man and Man* (The Mac-
millan company 1965), p. 97.

16. *Ibid.,* p. 30, and Buber, *I and Thou* (Clark edi-
tion), p. 75.

17. Paul Tillich, *Systematic Theology* (The University
of Chicago Press, 1951), Vol. I, p. 176.

18. *Ibid.,* p. 185.

19. *Ibid.,* p. 184. Elsewhere Tillich made the following comment about freedom and destiny: "Nobody is

free beyond the margin which his destiny leaves him. This margin is not very large, but it is continuously present, which makes it possible for us to be creative.

"Men have creative freedom. That is another element in it. Creation is a word which is originally used for God; but since what we use for God must have some analogy in us, we also experience creative moments. In creative moments we transcend the given, that which is given in us in this moment. This transcending the given happens in a centered reaction. And this centered reaction, then, is freedom." (James B. Ashbrook [ed.], "Paul Tillich in Conversation on Psychology and Theology," *Journal of Pastoral Care*, Vol. 3 [September 1972], p. 177.)

20. Carl R. Rogers, *On Becoming a Person* (Houghton Mifflin Company, 1961), p. 61.

21. Buber, *Between Man and Man*, p. 30.

22. Tillich, *Systematic Theology*, Vol. I, p. 184.

23. Charles F. Kemp, *A Pastoral Counseling Guidebook* (Abingdon Press, 1971), p. 91, citing D. W. Orr, *Professional Counseling on Human Behavior* (Franklin Watts, Inc., 1965), p. 111; Nathaniel Lehrman has also urged ministers to be more accepting of their sexual feelings because feelings are distinctive from behavior. "This discussion is of course based on the psychoanalytic concept that there is a fundamental difference between thoughts and deeds, and on the belief that while tender extramarital sexual thoughts and feelings are inevitable under certain circumstances, extramarital sexual deeds are not." (Lehrman, *loc. cit.*, p. 51.)

24. Tillich, *Systematic Theology*, Vol. I, p. 184.

25. Paul E. Johnson, *Psychology of Pastoral Care*, (Abingdon Press, 1953), pp. 96–97.

26. These sentences are from a section titled "Silence Which Is Communication." (Buber, *Between Man and Man*, pp. 3–4.)

27. John W. Drakeford, "The Budgeting of Time in Pastoral Counseling," in Wayne E. Oates (ed.), *An In-*

troduction to Pastoral Counseling (The Broadman Press, 1959), pp. 96–107; Wayne E. Oates, "The Time Element in Pastoral Counseling," in his *Protestant Pastoral Counseling* (The Westminster Press, 1962), pp. 101–116; Johnson, *Psychology of Pastoral Care*, pp. 82–84; Paul E. Johnson, *Person and Counselor* (Abingdon Press, 1967), pp. 179–180.

28. Clinebell, *Basic Types*, pp. 300–302; E. Mansell Pattison has also suggested: "Finally, one of the best methods for maintaining perspective in one's counseling relations is periodical review with a constructive critic. Thus the pastor might systematically share his pastoral care experiences with a reliable colleague, or in consultation with a professional psychotherapist. . . . An uninvolved third person has a unique vantage from which to detect distortions of the counseling relationship." (E. Mansell Pattison, "Transference and Countertransference in Pastoral Care," *Journal of Pastoral Care*, Vol. XIX, No. 4 [Winter 1965], pp. 201–202.)

29. Oates, *Protestant Pastoral Counseling*, p. 144.

30. Theodor Reik, *Of Love and Lust* (Farrar, Straus & Cudahy, Inc., 1957), p. 32.

31. Erwin Wexberg, *The Psychology of Sex* (Farrar and Rinehart, Inc., 1931), p. 110.

32. Hunt, *op. cit.*, pp. 80–81.

33. From personal correspondence between the author and Thomas McDill, June 20, 1973.

34. John A. Ordway, "Transference Reactions in Parishioners," *Journal of Pastoral Care*, Vol. XXIV (March 1970), p. 59.

35. Pattison, *loc. cit.*, pp. 198–199.

36. Clinebell, *Basic Types*, p. 31.

37. Herbert W. Stroup, Jr., and Norma Schweitzer Wood, *Sexuality and the Counseling Pastor* (Fortress Press, 1974), pp. 46–48.

38. See also Clinebell, *Basic Types*, "Crisis Counseling," Ch. 9.

39. Reuel L. Howe, *The Miracle of Dialogue* (The Seabury Press, Inc., 1963), p. 3.

40. Charlotte Holt Clinebell, *Meet Me in the Middle* (Harper & Row, Publishers, Inc., 1973), pp. 54 and 55.

41. William H. Masters and Virginia E. Johnson, "Why Women Have Sexual Fantasies," *Redbook Magazine*, Vol. 144 (February 1975), pp. 70 ff.